What you don't know can eat you

EVERYTHING YOU EVER WANTED TO KNOW ABOUT ZOMBIES

All zombie research is theoretical. We can never know exactly what the coming pandemic will look like until the teeming undead horde is finally at our doorsteps. Once the dead rise, the days of study and conjecture are over. Gone will be reasoned debate and hard scientific study. Gone will be global lines of communication and easy access to information. Gone will be the support structures that allow us to easily engage in serious scientific, social, and historic investigation.

When the dead rise, it's run-and-scream time.

*   *   *

"Matt Mogk is a walking catalog of important modern developments in zombie research, and his book is an essential resource in the coming zombie apocalypse."

—Michael Harris, PhD, professor of neuroscience,
University of Alaska, Fairbanks

"Pulling together key knowledge strands untapped by previous works of zombie scholarship, Matt Mogk is staking out essential new territory at the nexus of history, science, popular culture, and reality."

—Brendan Riley, PhD, assistant professor
of cultural studies, Columbia College Chicago

This title is also available as an eBook.

EVERYTHING WANTED TO

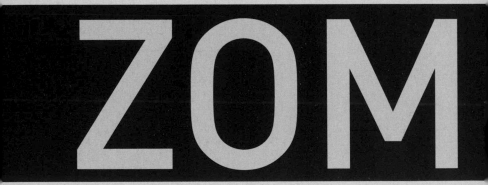

ZOM

GALLERY BOOKS

NEW YORK   LONDON   TORONTO   SYDNEY   NEW DELHI

MATT MOGK

YOU EVER
KNOW ABOUT

BIES

G

Gallery Books
A Division of Simon & Schuster, Inc.
1230 Avenue of the Americas
New York, NY 10020

First Gallery Books trade paperback edition September 2011

GALLERY BOOKS and colophon are registered trademarks
of Simon & Schuster, Inc.

For information about special discounts for bulk purchases,
please contact Simon & Schuster Special Sales at 1-866-506-1949
or business@simonandschuster.com.

The Simon & Schuster Speakers Bureau can bring authors to your
live event. For more information or to book an event, contact the
Simon & Schuster Speakers Bureau at 1-866-248-3049 or visit our
website at www.simonspeakers.com.

Designed by Akasha Archer

Manufactured in the United States of America

10 9 8 7 6 5 4 3 2 1

Library of Congress Cataloging-in-Publication Data

Mogk, Matt.
    Everything you ever wanted to know about zombies / Matt Mogk.
        p.   cm.
    1. Zombies. I. Title.
      GR581.M65 2011
      398.21—dc23
                                                        2011025020

ISBN 978-1-4516-4157-8
ISBN 978-1-4516-4158-5 (ebook)

To Bigman and PosMa

CONTENTS

ACKNOWLEDGMENTS

First and foremost, thanks to all the members of Zombie Research Society from around the world for sharing my passion for zombie science, survival, and pop culture. Without you, this project would never have gotten off the ground. In particular, special acknowledgement goes to Lisa Bolton and Mikey Taylor for helping keep ZRS headed in the right direction. And to John Farrell, Lisa Bane, Zoe Mora, Marcus Mooers, and the other dedicated local chapter leaders, both in the United States and abroad.

To the ZRS Advisory Board past and present, including Daniel Drezner, Scott Kenemore, Bradley Voytek, Timothy Verstynen, Brendan Riley, Mike Harris, and Peter Cummings, thank you for your commitment to the mission of cultivating zombie scholarship and respect in the arts and sciences. Additional recognition goes to Steven Schlozman for your enthusiasm and encouragement, and to George Romero for creating the monster that has become my obsession.

A special thank-you goes to Max Brooks for your important contributions to this book, your broad support, and your friendship.

I greatly appreciate the dozens of scholars, authors and artists who agreed to participate in this project, such as Robert Kirkman, William Stout, Paul Wernick, Rhett Reese, Matt Schantzen, Scott Bowen, Leif Becker, Josh Taylor, Lucas Culshaw, and Samuel Stebbins. Thanks to Frank Weimann for getting the process going, to Chris Easley for your thoughtful draft review, and to Jennifer Heddle for guiding it to a successful end.

And finally a debt of gratitude is owed to my friends and family for letting me endlessly go on about zombies, especially The Troll, who gets the brunt of it on a daily basis. Thanks to T for sounding the alarm and Majaraj for putting out fires at the finish line. To Grimm, Danger, and Annie, thanks for keeping me on my toes even though sometimes my toes get tired. Thanks to Don and Dianne for the American food. Thanks to my parents for pretty much everything.

But most of all thanks to Seamus for hanging in until I got things figured out.

FOREWORD

by Max Brooks

If you don't know anything about zombies but you'd like to learn, this is the book for you. That's how Matt explained his new project to me. Everyone knows that zombies are popular, but what exactly *are* zombies? Are they the voodoo slaves that obey arcane wizards in Haiti? Are they the flesh-eating hordes that star in so many apocalyptic movies? Are they the singing, campy, well-choreographed cadavers of Michael Jackson's "Thriller"? The answer to each of those questions is yes.

The zombie subgenre has recently achieved pandemic status, with a horde of books, movies, TV shows, comics, video games, and yes, even apps invading every corner of our daily lives. For many years, there has been a strict line dividing dedicated fans who study every frame of *Dawn of the Dead* like it's the Zapruder film, and the rest of the world, who scratch their heads in wonder. That line between fans and "civilians" seemed uncrossable—until now.

Matt Mogk once walked away from success, and that's why I offered to write this foreword. Yes, he's way into zombies, and he's carved out an impressive niche as one of the foremost experts of the age. But for me, the path that led him to this new career is easily as interesting as the career itself. A long time ago, probably when he still had hair, Matt worked for a Hollywood literary management company. To say that it was a frustrating, depressing, utterly confounding profession would be an understatement. So many writers, so little talent. Even more mind-boggling than the limitless excrement he forced on the marketplace was the insatiable appetite the marketplace had for it. Like the lone Wall Street trader who wrestles with the logic of credit default swaps or the Washington intern who loses sleep over campaign finance loopholes, Matt found himself being pulled through a machine that was slowly, steadily grinding his spirit into dust.

One day he was charged with hawking a particularly noxious turd to a studio executive who was looking for something completely different. "I want a family script," this "creative executive" demanded, "like *101 Dalmatians* but without the dogs"! The script in Matt's charge, an adult thriller set in South America, could not have been less suited to the parameters placed before him. Frustrated, demoralized, and teetering at the edge of his moral abyss, Matt responded with a confident "That's EXACTLY what this script is about! I'll send it right over first thing tomorrow, and trust me, you'll LOVE it!" And he did. And *they* did! Score one—one BIG one—for the new super-manager Matt Mogk, the man who could sell anything . . . except his soul. *If this is what it means to succeed,* Matt told himself, *then I don't want any part of it.*

So he walked away from a newly white-hot career as a Hollywood dung salesman and several years later was standing on the set of the Spike TV series *Deadliest Warrior.* This new Matt Mogk was now the founder and president of the Zombie Research Society, an organization devoted to the study and promotion of all things living dead. That's where we became friends: planning our strategy for the show's "Zombie vs. Vampire" episode. We'd met a few months earlier at the nation's first dedicated zombie convention (yes, there is one now), and at the time, I wasn't sure what to make of him. Given the growing popularity of zombies, and the growing ranks of those seeking to make a quick buck off them, I was deeply suspicious. However, I was wrong (as is usually the case in my life).

Matt not only turned out to be a stand-up guy, but he is legitimately, deeply, inspiringly passionate about the subculture of the living dead. As we sat in the green room of *Deadliest Warrior*, building our case for a zombie victory over vampirism, I could only marvel at the inner workings of the mind of Mogk. I've often said that I think about zombies way too much, and compared to most people, I do. I've considered their physiology, their behavioral patterns, the threat they pose to us as a species, and the steps we might take to protect ourselves from them. *Publishers Weekly* once dubbed my first book, *The Zombie Survival Guide*, as "unnecessarily exhaustive." They had yet to learn what those words really meant!

Unlike me, Matt has also considered the cultural impact of zombie fiction on the human psyche, deconstructing it like an NYU film school professor might deconstruct the works of postmodern French cinema. Somehow he's managed to keep a toe in both universes. Matt can easily jump into the zombie sandbox for a heated argument about what sword works best against undead necks, then jump right back out for an intellectual analysis of the later works of George Romero.

If zombieism were a religion, I would be a monk, sequestered behind walls of books and ruminations, while Matt would be a pilgrim, out among the people, preaching, educating, and converting from dawn till dusk. When he told me he was writing a book "for people who don't know anything about zombies but would like to learn," my only thought was: "We couldn't have a better ambassador."

So if you are someone who's never given the living dead

much thought but are curious as to why the living living can't get enough of them, then this is your book. You may be captivated, or repelled, or just plain weirded out by its pages, but by its end, the one thing you won't be any longer is ignorant. Prepare to become a zombie expert.

Oh yeah, and don't read it before going to bed.

SECTION I

ZOMBIE BASICS

After a typically harsh Chicago winter, the city by the lake was sunny and bright in the early summer months of 1969. Escaping the rising afternoon heat, a young film critic named Roger Ebert ducked into a local neighborhood theater to catch the matinee. He found an empty seat among the packed audience of mostly children and families and settled in for what he expected to be just another low-budget monster movie called *Night of the Living Dead*.

Though the film had already generated some negative buzz, with *Variety* going so far as to call it an orgy of violence,[1] Ebert was consciously withholding judgment until he watched it for himself. He took his new job seriously, and having grown up a huge science fiction and horror fan, he was sure to be more open to the charms of this black-and-white screamer than some stuffy reviewer from the East Coast. After all, how different could it be from the hundreds of other formulaic B-movies he'd seen in the last decade?

The room went dark, the movie projector sputtered to life, and Ebert's question was answered in the first few minutes of grainy footage that splashed across the screen. This film was not only different; it was unlike anything he'd ever seen before:

> There was almost complete silence. The movie had long ago stopped being delightfully scary, and had become unexpectedly terrifying. A little girl across the aisle from me, maybe nine years old, was sitting very still in her seat and crying.
>
> I don't think the younger kids really knew what hit them. They'd seen horror movies before, but this was something else. This was ghouls eating people—you could actually see what they were eating. This was little girls killing their mothers. This was being set on fire. Worst of all, nobody got out alive—even the hero got killed.[2]

The gruesome new monsters in writer/director George A. Romero's terrifying vision gave audiences such a shock that many were literally afraid to leave their seats after the closing credits ran and the lights went up. People freaked out. They covered their eyes, clung to the arms of complete strangers, and screamed at the top of their lungs for the nightmare to end. Then when it finally did, they turned around, bought another ticket, and went back in for more.

The modern zombie was born.

1: DEFINITION OF A ZOMBIE

The *Oxford English Dictionary* is widely regarded as the premier dictionary of the English language and is rated the most comprehensive dictionary on the planet by Guinness World Records. It includes specific definitions for countless obscure and unusual monsters, including the infamous chupacabra of Latin America and Bigfoot's Himalayan cousin, the albino yeti. But it does not include an accurate definition of the modern zombie. It instead focuses solely on the slavellke zombie of Afro-Haitian tradition that is completely unrelated to the modern zombie of contemporary pop culture.

---

zombie (zom-bie)

pronunciation: zämbē

1. A corpse said to be revived by witchcraft, especially in certain African and Caribbean religions.
2. A mixed drink consisting of several kinds of rum, liqueur, and fruit juice.

Informal:
— A person who is or appears to be lifeless, apathetic, or completely unresponsive to his or her surroundings.
— A computer controlled by another person without the owner's knowledge and used for sending spam or other illegal or illicit activities.

Unfortunately, the *Encyclopaedia Britannica* is no better. A search for *zombie* only turns up results for the Haitian zombie and the zombie computer. Not exactly what you might call encyclopedic results.

Does this mean that every movie, video game, event, and organization that this book focuses on simply doesn't exist? Are the tens of millions of people who participate in zombie walks, zombie proms, zombie pub crawls, zombie conventions, and zombie film festivals across the planet gathered to express their interest in a nonthing? Or, instead, is the modern zombie being overlooked? It seems that billions of dollars in annual revenue across multiple platforms still can't put the modern zombie officially on the map.

Based on an extensive study of the modern zombie's evolution over the past half century and on countless interviews with zombie fans and scholars across the globe, here is the first and most authoritative definition:

> *The modern zombie is a relentlessly aggressive, reanimated human corpse driven by a biological infection.*

This definition is intended to be narrow enough to clearly identify the modern zombie's unique characteristics and broad enough to apply equally to the original *Night of the Living Dead* as to the zombie films being conceived and produced today. Furthermore, by breaking down the definition into its component parts, three key elements emerge against which all manner of creature can be quickly and easily judged.

These three definitional elements of the modern zombie are (1) it is a reanimated human corpse, (2) it is relentlessly aggressive, and (3) it is biologically infected and infectious.

(1) HUMAN CORPSE

Zombies occupy the decaying shell of what was once human. They inhabit corpses of flesh, blood, and bone, which makes their systems imperfect. So while they may be relentlessly determined, they are far from invincible. Zombies have a limited life span, given that their bodies are rotting as human corpses do, and they operate under the same laws of science and reason that all worldly beings must operate under.

(2) RELENTLESSLY AGGRESSIVE

Whether the undead scourge is created and spread by bite, by blood, by radiation, or on the wind, zombies are first and foremost defined by their relentless aggression. You can't negotiate with a zombie. You can't tell a zombie what to do. A zombie has single-minded focus. It will never stop. It will never surrender. A zombie will continue to move toward its goal at any cost.

Let Sleeping Corpses Lie (1974)

DOCTOR: Are you hurt?

GEORGE: No, but it tried its hardest. What the hell's wrong with it?

DOCTOR: We don't know. It's the third one born since yesterday with an incredible aggressiveness, almost homicidal in its intensity.

---

(3) BIOLOGICAL INFECTION

The modern zombie is biological in nature, not supernatural or magical. This unique characteristic allows it to be studied from a scientific perspective and is also an essential element in our understanding of how the condition of being a zombie occurs. The prevailing theory is that the zombie state is transmitted by an infectious contagion that readily spreads to new hosts. We call it the coming zombie pandemic.

KNOW YOUR ZOMBIES: BILL HINZMAN

Night of the Living Dead (1968)

Known as the Cemetery Zombie, actor Bill Hinzman played the first-ever modern zombie to appear anywhere when he lurched on the screen in the opening moments of *Night of the Living Dead*. As part of George Romero's core production team on that film, his name will forever be linked to the iconic monster he helped bring to life.

Hinzman worked behind the camera with Romero on future projects before writing, directing, and starring in a lackluster rip-off of *Night* called *FleshEater* in 1988.

ILLUSTRATION BY JOSH TAYLOR

2: VOODOO ZOMBIES

Romero didn't think the flesh eaters he created were zombies because prior to *Night of the Living Dead* the world only knew zombies to be soulless slaves of the Haitian voodoo tradition, magically brought back from the dead to do the bidding of their masters, usually as menial labor. In fact, other than their shared name, there is no connection between the voodoo zombie and the modern zombie.

Unlike actual corpses rising from the grave, voodoo zombies are induced through a mixture of drugs, religious ritual, cultural belief, and spiritual possession. After being put into a trancelike state that approximates a coma, victims awaken and are told that their souls have been taken from their bodies. Then, to keep them under control, they are regularly fed the hallucinogenic drug datura, also known as the "zombie cucumber."

Wade Davis is a world-renowned anthropologist best known for his 1985 book *The Serpent and the Rainbow*, which explores the zombie traditions of Haitian voodoo. The book was made into a movie of the same name in 1988 that took great liberties with the original text. Saying that Davis hated the adaptation is an understatement. He's gone as far as to declare it to be the worst movie ever made in the history of Hollywood. Davis isn't right about that. *Serpent* isn't even the worst movie of 1988. If you have any doubts, pick up a copy of *Mac and Me*, a shameless knockoff of *E.T.* featuring an extended dance montage in a McDonald's parking lot.

I can't help but feel a little sorry for Wade Davis, because he, like George Romero, understands that the flesh eaters of *Night of the Living Dead* should never have been called zombies in the first place:

> *The zombies in movies like* Night of the Living Dead *have no connection at all to the zombie of Haiti. It is not a correct or fair use of that word.*[3]

Davis knows what he's talking about. He earned a PhD from Harvard, was the 2009 recipient of the Royal Canadian Geographical Society's Gold Medal, and has been a featured speaker at the TED Conference, where geniuses and world leaders go to shape the future of our planet. At the same time, he's spent the last thirty years explaining that voodoo zombies don't want to eat your brains. It's got to be a little frustrating.

But Davis has an unassailable point. From a dramatic standpoint, there is no connection between the voodoo zombie and the modern zombie. From a factual, anthropological, religious, or historic standpoint, there is no connection between the voodoo zombie and the modern zombie. It's as misguided as asserting that the protective cup that athletes stuff in their jocks when playing contact sports is closely related to a coffee cup because they share the same name. And then using that as justification to include the athletic cup in an academic study of the history of the Peruvian coffee bean.

AT THE MOVIES

In the 1960s, zombies were not on the popular-culture radar. Two notable books were published about Hollywood film monsters that decade, and neither even mentioned zombies. *A Pictorial History of Hollywood Film Monsters* and *Master Movie*  *Monsters* feature mummies, vampires, aliens, werewolves, and even mad scientists, but zombies don't get a single word of coverage. Zombies were omitted not because they weren't getting the respect they deserved but, rather, because *Night of the Living Dead* hadn't yet been made.

Haitian zombies were known in anthropological circles, but they certainly weren't considered a bankable film subgenre. The few voodoo zombies on-screen in the 1930s and 1940s were not inherently dangerous and took aggressive action only when instructed to do so by their masters. In fact, they were so docile and fundamentally good that they often turned on those same masters when ordered to do something particularly nefarious. They could even, as Wade Davis explores in *The Serpent and the Rainbow*, talk about their memories and experiences with pathos and recognize themselves as individuals participating in their community's culture.

Even in Hollywood versions of Haitian voodoo zombie stories, zombies weren't scary. In the 1932 film *White Zombie*, they're described as "corpses taken from their graves and made to work in sugar mills and the fields at night." That is what they were in the movies before *Night of the Living Dead*, and that is how they are still perceived in Haiti today.

The Serpent and the Rainbow (1988)

DR. ALAN: I need you to remember what happened before you died.

ZOMBIE: I remember it all. The coffin, the burial, I saw it all.

DR. ALAN: Were you sick? What was it that you felt?

ZOMBIE: I heard the dirt falling on me. The darkness pressed me down, down.

IN THE FLESH

Of all the differences between voodoo zombies of the Afro-Haitian tradition and the modern zombie as first realized by George Romero, none is more striking or more overlooked than the fact that voodoo zombies are not dead. Let me repeat: voodoo zombies are not dead. They are as alive as you or I but operate under the strong religious or substance-induced belief that they have been brought back from the dead to serve a living master.

Webster University professor emeritus Bob Corbett has studied Haitian culture for decades and personally traveled to Haiti more than fifty times over the past fifteen years to investigate its people and traditions. He writes:

> *Eating the zombie cucumber keeps them in their zonked-out state, but otherwise they are just like animals in a pen and will do what they are told to do. Mainly they're used as slave labor.*

In our correspondence, Corbett went on to emphasize that voodoo zombies have beating hearts and normal blood flow and body temperature. They need to sleep, eat regular foods, and eliminate waste like the rest of us, and they are not contagious or aggressive.

There are people in Haiti today who believe that they have been transformed into zombies, but they still retain the same rights as any other citizen. If a zombie is killed or its death is caused through the neglect of another, the offender is put on trial for murder. As I said, voodoo zombies aren't dead. They are also not aggressive, nor created by a biological infection. The lack of connection between the voodoo zombie and the modern zombie cannot be overstated.

3: ZOMBIE EVOLUTION

The modern zombie first appeared in *Night of the Living Dead* in 1968. Made on a shoestring budget with borrowed cars and part-time actors, *Night* tells the story of a group of strangers trapped in an isolated farmhouse while roaming zombies try to break through their hasty defenses and eat them.

As the film opens, two siblings, Johnny and Barbra, arrive at a remote cemetery to visit their long-dead father's grave. Johnny realizes that Barbra is as spooked to be there as she was when they were kids. He teases her, pointing to an old man wandering across the grass and playing into her fright by suggesting that the guy is an attacker. The joke is on Johnny, though. The wanderer is actually a risen flesh eater bearing down on them. Johnny will be dead just seconds after his naively prophetic words.

Night of the Living Dead (1968)

JOHNNY: They're coming to get you, Barbra.

BARBRA: Stop it. You're ignorant.

JOHNNY: They're coming for you, Barbra.

BARBRA: Stop it. You're acting like a child.

JOHNNY: They're coming for you. Look! There comes one now!

Night brought in an estimated $42 million worldwide. When adjusted for inflation, George Romero's tiny independent film grossed the equivalent of nearly $265 million in today's dollars. That's more than double the box-office numbers of 2009's smash hit zombie comedy *Zombieland*, prompting one critic to exclaim that the film had been given a license to print money.[4]

Despite its mass appeal, critics were slow to come around, but eventually the groundbreaking nature of Romero's horror masterpiece couldn't be ignored. *New York Times* reviewer Vincent Canby snidely referred to the film as junk in 1970,[5] but by 2004 the *Times* did an about-face, including *Night of the Living Dead* on a list of top pictures in the history of cinema. Now regarded as one of the most influential films in modern horror, *Night* is among a highly selective collection of pictures archived in the National Film Registry at the United States Library of Congress for its profound cultural, historical, and aesthetic significance.

When one speaks of zombie movies today, one is really speaking of movies that are either made by or directly influenced by one man: director George A. Romero.

—Gospel of the Living Dead *(2006), Kim Paffenroth, PhD*

And just how important is the man behind the film? According to award-winning writer-director Quentin Tarantino, George Romero is single-handedly responsible for all the action, gore, and intensity that make modern genre films great.[6] Max Brooks, bestselling author of *Zombie Survival Guide* and *World War Z*, says that when it comes to the modern zombie, it's Romero's world, and we're all just living in it. And John Carpenter, director of such horror classics as *Halloween* (1978) and *The Thing* (1982), simply states that Romero profoundly influenced an entire culture.[7]

The same year as *Night*'s release, legendary actor Boris Karloff, who played the title character in dozens of monster classics such as *Frankenstein* and *The Mummy*, prophetically observed, "My kind of horror isn't horror anymore."[8] He was right. *Night of the Living Dead* had changed things forever.

BORN FROM VAMPIRES

So where did Romero get his idea for the modern zombie? Jump back to 1953 and Richard Matheson, a young paperback writer with two twenty-five-cent novels to his name. The prestigious Nelson Doubleday Company had just agreed to publish his first hardcover, a work of vampire fiction called *I Am Legend*. Set in contemporary Los Angeles, *Legend* didn't rehash Old World interpretations of the iconic monsters but instead turned them from elegant loners who lived on the fringes of society into a horde of bloodthirsty ghouls violently driven to suck the last drops of life from every living person on earth.

Romero was so inspired by the book that when he decided to make his first film some fourteen years later, he set out to create a loose adaptation of *I Am Legend*. In fact, Romero's and Matheson's stories are so similar that Matheson initially mistook *Night of the Living Dead* for his own work:

> I caught that on television, and I said to myself, "Wait a minute—did they make another version of I Am Legend *they didn't tell me about?"* Later they told me Romero did it as an homage, which means he gets it for nothing![9]

Though *Legend* has been directly adapted to the big screen three times, most recently as a Will Smith blockbuster,[10] many argue that *Night of the Living Dead* is a truer interpretation of Matheson's vision than any of the official versions. But what sets Romero's film apart from *I Am Legend*, what makes it truly great, is Romero's deliberate rejection of all aspects of the vampire myth in favor of a much scarier, much more realistic threat.

Although Romero decided against having the undead transform into vampires after their death, the stumbling, staggering corpses in his film do bite people and eat their flesh; and, vampire-like, their bloody victims become undead cannibals as a result of becoming involuntary meals.
—Real Zombies (2010), Brad Steiger

Matheson's goal was to bring the vampire into the modern age by creating a biological explanation for its existence. He invented a bacterial infection that created vampires, *Bacilli vampiri*, which could then be scientifically researched and understood. Matheson's vampires could no longer fly or transfigure themselves. They didn't have superhuman strength, and they didn't turn into bats. But Matheson carried over several elements of the traditional vampire myth. His vampires still hated crosses and Christian symbols. They couldn't tolerate exposure to garlic. They died in direct sunlight and could be killed using a wooden stake through the heart. Romero rejected this cultural baggage.

By creating the flesh eater, a creature that literally arose in the modern age with no limiting Carpathian Mountain mythology, Romero was able to remove all of the Old World superstition and give birth to a completely scientific monster. No myth, just pure biology. No special powers, just the limited humanlike abilities of a rotting corpse. No supernatural force, just the logical result of modern man's polluting impact on the natural world. Still, the relationship between Romero's flesh eaters and Matheson's vampires remains the closest that the modern zombie has to any other creature.

FLESH EATERS LURCH FORTH

As you might expect, given the history of Romero's connection to *I Am Legend*, he didn't consider the creatures he created to be zombies at all. He called them flesh eaters.

In fact, Romero was so dedicated to the brand-new concept of his flesh-eating monster that he originally named his film *Night of the Flesh Eaters*. It was only in the eleventh hour that the distribution company swapped in *Living Dead* for *Flesh Eaters* in hopes of appealing to a wider audience.[11] At the time, *living dead* was a term used broadly to refer to various undead monsters, including vampires, mummies, and even Frankenstein. By way of example, *Cave of the Living Dead* (1965), *Fangs of the Living Dead* (1968), and *Crypt of the Living Dead* (1972) were all released around the same time as Romero's *Night*, and all are vampire movies. The title was changed so late and in such a rush that on Wednesday, November 1, 1968, one month after its official premiere, a *Pittsburgh Gazette* review still referred to the film as *Night of the Flesh Eaters*.

So how did we get from flesh eaters to living dead to the entire planet calling Romero's monsters zombies? It was a slow ten-year process, culminating in yet another distribution company changing the name of yet another Romero film.

In 1978, Romero was approached by famed horror director Dario Argento, who offered to bankroll his next film, giving Romero $750,000 cash as long as Argento could have the

European rights.[12] Argento then changed the name of Romero's second flesh-eater movie from *Dawn of the Dead* to *Zombi*. Presto, the label stuck. The film raked in $55 million worldwide, becoming arguably even more iconic than *Night*, and that's how we all came to mistakenly believe that Romero's flesh eaters were zombies.

THE SICKNESS EVOLVES

The modern zombie has remained remarkably consistent since it first lurched into popular consciousness in 1968. Most films follow a basic plot structure that is very close, if not identical, to that of *Night of the Living Dead*. But there are certain qualities or aspects of zombies that have changed over the decades. Most notable is the process by which a human is turned into a flesh eater.

Romero's original vision was that zombies were not contagious. They were created by an infection present in the environment, not spread from zombie to human. Anyone who dies for any reason will acquire it. According to Romero, a bite is not necessary to transmit the infection, and he remains true to this original conception and uses this approach in all of his zombie films. It was Romero himself, though, who unintentionally opened the door to a new interpretation of how zombies are created. In *Night of the Living Dead*, the first person to turn from human to zombie on-screen is a little girl. She has been bitten on the arm and is suffering some strange illness. The bite doesn't appear to be substantial enough to cause any real damage, but the girl is barely conscious, and she soon dies and comes back as a zombie.

This terrifying turn of events sends a clear message: bites

matter. They're toxic at the very least and at worst may be directly related to becoming a zombie and spreading the plague. In Romero's second zombie film, *Dawn of the Dead*, the two main characters who expire and return as zombies both die as a result of bite wounds. Though Romero has made his perspective clear over the years, the genie was out of the bottle.

Popular understanding accepted Romero's idea that the zombie condition is caused by an infectious plague, but the spread of the plague was narrowed to include only those who have been directly infected by a zombie bite or exposure to zombie blood or body fluid. Not only does the current zombie-contagion model align more closely with its vampire roots, but it also conforms to our knowledge of infectious diseases, allowing zombie outbreaks to dramatically mirror more common outbreaks such as swine flu, mad cow, and rabies. The zombie sickness doesn't automatically afflict everyone, but we all have the potential to be infected if exposed

4: LIVING ZOMBIES

A lab experiment goes horribly wrong, and a new virus is unleashed on the population, turning those infected into bloodthirsty maniacs driven by pure rage and capable of running at full speed. This is the premise of *28 Days Later,* the 2002 hit British film that introduced the most popular advancements in the subgenre of zombie films since George Romero invented the modern zombie in 1968. It also sparked a heated debate among enthusiasts about what exactly constitutes a zombie and how fast is too fast for the ghoulish horde to move.

28 Days Later was groundbreaking as a low-budget horror film because of its immense mainstream success, but its core concept of a communicable rage infection was nothing new. A lesser-known film released seventeen years earlier, *Warning Sign*, depicts an accident in a secure lab that exposes workers to a deadly toxin that attacks the rage center of their brains, driving them to hunt and kill those not infected. Sound familiar?

The premise of the two films is almost identical, with the main difference being that *Warning*'s infection is airborne and contained within the boundaries of a secure research facility, while the *28 Days* infection is transferred by direct fluid contact to the entire population of Britain.

Warning Sign (1985)

CAL: Make it simple. What are you saying?

DAN: It drives people crazy, that's what I'm saying. Soldiers turn on their comrades. Civilian victims murder their doctors, and then they die. That's what's going on in that building right now.

CAL: I don't believe it. This is deliberate?

So why did *Warning Sign* hardly make a splash in the popular evolution of the modern zombie when *28 Days Later* completely turned the subgenre on its head?

From an execution standpoint, *Warning* is a relatively forgettable effort. Hal Barwood, its writer-director, has yet to make another movie. *28 Days*, however, was the first big hit in Danny Boyle's directing career (although his 1996 film, *Trainspotting*, enjoyed some success at the box office and in critical reviews). He went on to win an Oscar for *Slumdog Millionaire* in 2008. But could there be something more at play? Could the key to the popularity of *28 Days Later* and its particular significance to the development of modern zombies lie in its quintessential zombieness?

Unlike those in *Warning*, the infected hordes in *28 Days* behave like rabid animals, unable to speak or reason. They will stop at nothing to accomplish their simple mission of finding and destroying every last surviving human on the planet. Though they don't eat the living, they do bite, scratch, and claw to transmit their deadly infection, much as conventional modern zombies do. They also lack any sense of individual identity or distinguishing characteristics, leading most to classify the picture as a zombie film despite the fact that no one ever comes back from the dead.

THE "ZOMBIES" OF *28 DAYS*

I first met Danny Boyle in the mid-1990s when he gave a talk at New York University in support of his first feature film, *Shallow Grave*. It's an indie suspense thriller about greed, madness, and roommates killing each other. The movie develops an impressive sense of tension, so I cornered Boyle after the screening and asked if he'd ever considered making a horror film, more specifically a zombie movie. He emphatically said no, that he had no interest in the zombie subgenre whatsoever. Jump forward eight years, and *28 Days Later* was raking in upward of $85 million at the box office, putting Boyle solidly on the map as a bankable director.

But if you ask Boyle today, he will still tell you he's never made a zombie movie. He doesn't see the rage-filled humans he created in *28 Days Later* as modern zombies. Zombie purists would agree with Boyle, arguing that a zombie that is still alive is not a zombie at all. Technically, they're correct.

If we look at our three criteria for the modern zombie, the third stipulates that a zombie is a reanimated human corpse. By this standard, the infected freaks of *28 Days Later* don't qualify. Living zombies are by definition not undead. They can be killed by stopping their hearts, and once dead, they do not come back to life as conventional zombies. In this way, they are fundamentally different from Romero's original vision of the flesh eater raised from the grave to feast on the living. Even the title, *28 Days Later*, refers to how long it takes for the rage-filled humans in Boyle's film to become so starved and dehydrated that they die out. Modern zombies don't starve, and they don't become dehydrated in any human sense of the word.

But what Danny Boyle essentially did with *28 Days Later* was to create the living zombie—and in doing so, he revolutionized the zombie subgenre, introducing a whole new arena for characterizing zombies and for zombie storytelling.

Like their undead counterparts, living zombies are biologically infected, relentlessly aggressive, and no longer cognizant individuals. If we set the definition of the modern zombie next to a definition of the living zombie, we can see how well the infected of *28 Days* qualify and how similar the two types are.

Here is the modern zombie:

The modern zombie is a relentlessly aggressive reanimated human corpse driven by a biological infection.

And here's the living zombie:

The living zombie is a relentlessly aggressive human driven by a biological infection.

The brilliance—and the original core quality—of Romero's flesh eaters is that they are grounded in science and reason rather than superstition and myth. The living zombie conforms to this core quality. If the infected maniac lumbering down the street looks like a zombie, bites like a zombie, and is contagious like a zombie, then for all intents and purposes, it's zombie enough for most.

At this point, thanks to Boyle's blockbuster innovation, living zombies are firmly ensconced in the zombie film subgenre.

 The 2009 film *Zombieland*, for example, introduced a raving horde that appears ambiguously living, or perhaps ambiguously dead. The movie seems to intentionally gloss over the monsters' life status, making it less relevant. *Zombieland*'s creatures

are identified by name as zombies, are ravenously hungry for human flesh, and have a pale, corpselike appearance. Many film scholars and fans alike believe them to be undead, but the only character to turn from human to flesh eater does so off-camera, making it unclear whether she died and came back to life or just went violently insane.

To get the final word, I spoke with the film's writing team of Rhett Reese and Paul Wernick, who confirmed that their zombies are indeed alive. They need to eat and drink water and can be killed like any other living person. Gone is the requisite focus on destroying the zombie brain to kill it, and gone is the concept of the dead rising. But almost anyone will tell you that *Zombieland* is a zombie movie. With a name like that, how could it not be?

Like rabid sickos, these zombies are living humans infected with a virus—but the zombie infection is incurable, and it transforms its victims into the same mindless, soulless creatures seen in zombie movies of decades past.
—Zombie Movies *(2008)*, Glenn Kay

FAST VS. SLOW

The most striking difference between Romero's flesh eaters and Boyle's rage-filled maniacs is not their status as living or dead but their speed. Before *28 Days Later,* zombies had always  been shambling and stiff. Sure, they'd speed up a bit when they were within striking distance of a meal, but for the most part, they walked at a snail's pace. Because Boyle kept his zombies alive, he was able to logically make them sprint, adding the advantage of speed to their traditional attributes of being relentlessly aggressive and highly contagious.

Some argue that speeding up the ghouls takes away from the classic gnawing anticipation of a shambling horde that can't win any footraces but always gets you in the end. True or not, the concept of fast zombies was such a hit that when it came time for a big-budget remake of Romero's classic *Dawn of the Dead* in 2004, the zombies were virtual track stars. But this time, they were also undead, so their speed couldn't be explained away by arguing that they were in some way still human. Zombie traditionalists who reluctantly accepted Boyle's contribution to the subgenre were up in arms when the actual dead ran, including Romero himself.

"They can't run! That's the other thing I insist on. *28 Days Later* I can forgive, because they're not dead; they're infected with some kind of a virus, so they're still human, therefore they are still capable of moving fast. That *Dawn of the Dead* remake, Christ, what did they do, get up from the dead and immediately take up a membership at a gym?"[13]

Simon Pegg is the writer and star of 2003's hit British zombie comedy *Shaun of the Dead* and a vocal advocate for the slow, shambling zombie over its faster counterpart seen in many recent movies. In a 2008 opinion piece published in the UK national newspaper *The Guardian*, Pegg strongly argues against sprinting zombies:

A biological agent, I'll buy. Some sort of super-virus? Sure, why not. But death? Death is a disability, not a superpower.

It's hard to run with a cold, let alone the most debilitating malady of them all.

Ironically, Pegg himself may have played a pivotal role in the rise of the fast zombie in cinema by poking fun at how easy their slower cousins are to avoid and annihilate in *Shaun of the Dead*. Director Zack Snyder said that he chose to make his ghouls run in the *Dawn of the Dead* remake, released one year after *Shaun*, not because of the infected in *28 Days Later* but because it's not so easy to make fun of a faster ghoul.

Whatever your preference, it's clear that both the slow and the fast zombie, both living and undead, are here to stay. As a traditionalist, I find it a challenge to accept. But diversity is usually a very good thing—or in this case, a very deadly thing. They walk, they run. They're alive, they're dead.

They're all after you just the same.

KNOW YOUR ZOMBIES: THE PRIEST

28 Days Later (2002)

Jim wakes up in an abandoned hospital, walks outside, and finds London mysteriously empty. He wanders the streets, searching for answers. In the graffiti-marked halls of a local church Jim finds a seemingly helpful priest who turns out to be a raving maniac. He quickly learns that in a zombie plague nowhere is safe.

With the Priest, *28 Days Later* ushered in the new era of living zombies, the biggest innovation in the zombie subgenre since Romero's *Night of the Living Dead*.

ILLUSTRATION BY JORELL RIVERA

5: VAMPIRES

As we've seen, vampires are so closely related to the modern zombie that they deserve their own chapter. After all, the modern zombie evolved from the vampire, and both share several defining characteristics: they are undead, they bite, and they consume humans in one way or another.

The obvious reason vampires aren't zombies is that, well, they're vampires. Principally, this means that they are not generally understood to be scientific or biological in nature. They have supernatural strength and speed, and according to various traditions, they can shapeshift into any number of other creatures. They can live forever, never decaying or growing old, and are nearly invincible as long as they avoid sunlight and never skip naptime. Scientifically speaking, vampires don't make a whole lot of sense.

Contemporary vampire writers have tried to pull the vampire into the modern age with various updates, including making them cool high school kids who sparkle or making them more like zombies, meaning more scientifically based. In *I Am Legend*, Richard Matheson provided biological explanations for his vampires. Remnants of Matheson's efforts to give vampires a scientific rationale can be seen in Will Smith's 2007 blockbuster adaptation of the book. In fact, *Legend*'s filmmakers intentionally tried to cash in on the popularity of zombies by giving vampires some of their qualities. But make no mistake, it's not a zombie movie.

Like vampires of old, the creatures that infect Smith's *I Am Legend* can leap over cars in a single bound. They magically climb on ceilings, they can scheme and strategize, and they sleep the days away in creepy clusters like bats. The plot pretends to hinge on a biological plague that can be cured someday, but repeated lapses in logic show a certain lack of respect for that premise.

Last Man on Earth (1964)

ROBERT: You'd prefer us to believe in vampires?

BEN: If they exist, yes. There are stories being told, Bob.

ROBERT: By people who are out of their minds with fear.

BEN: But there are too many to be coincidental, stories about people who have died and come back.

ROBERT: They're just stories!

This tendency to blur the lines between vampire and zombie—to associate the two in confused ways or borrow from zombies to enhance vampires—is actually widespread. Ultimately, the connection between ancient vampire traditions and the modern zombie is tenuous at best. But several well-known examples are worth mentioning, if for no other reason than to show the distinct differences between the modern zombie and the vampire. Here is a brief tour of the most prominent vampire traditions that pop up in zombie books.

THE NACHZEHRER

According to Germanic lore, the Nachzehrer occupies the corpse of a person who died in extreme circumstances, such as suicide, murder, or violent accident. In the case of a deadly infectious disease passing through the region, the first person to die of the illness was thought likely to turn into a Nachzehrer.

Similar to the modern zombie, Nachzehrers do eat human flesh, but they don't restrict their diet to the living. They were thought to chew their own hands, legs, and clothing while still inside the grave. After crawling out, they would eat the bodies of the other dead in the cemetery, giving them a superior ick factor but little cultural cachet.

The Nachzehrer does not just attack the living. Instead, just as he gnaws off his own dead flesh, he also eats from the clothing and the flesh of neighboring corpses.
—Der Werwolf (1862), Wilhelm Hertz

Unlike zombies, Nachzehrers don't spread their affliction to others through a bite or fluid transfer. The legends of the Nachzehrers are essentially the German version of the vampire legends of Eastern Europe. Like vampires, Nachzehrers were believed to return from the grave with the specific goal of attacking family members and other friends and acquaintances.

THE REVENANT

A revenant can be a variety of entities, from something as ethereal as a ghost to the physical presence of the walking corpse. Either way, its mission is to torment the living, but revenants usually have specific targets in mind: people they knew when they were living. As vampire expert Scott Bowen explains, the revenant is a creature that reflects the conflicts or losses of particular human relationships:

This likely arises out of the psychological trauma caused by the death of a close relative. One of Tolstoy's two famous vampire stories is about a father returning home to his family from war as a vampire.

Bowen adds that a person who died in dire circumstances, such as from a terrible disease or some violent act, increases the family's suffering. This grief and trauma ultimately gets expressed as a cultural fear that the victim will rise from the dead.

Revenants prey on humans, but this could mean any range of behaviors from blood drinking or eating flesh to simply causing stress through perpetual haunting. Bowen notes that the term *revenant* occurs often in the context of vampire stories throughout that creature's long literary history. The two are apparently very closely related.

THE CHINESE VAMPIRE

The Chiang-Shih is a legendary Chinese creature with striking similarities to our modern understanding of the vampire. Much like the Nachzehrer, the Chinese vampire was a human who died violently. Suicides, murder victims, drowning victims, and the hanged were believed to be transformed easily if left unburied.

The Chiang-Shih is nocturnal and very violent, often ripping apart its victims and pulling off their heads and limbs. It also possesses a strong sexual drive and often attacks women, raping and killing them. Repeated attacks on humans build up the strength of the Chiang-Shih until it is able to shape-shift into a wolf or a flying beast.

Finally, like both the Nachzehrer and the revenant, the Chiang-Shih is a single entity. It doesn't travel in groups or carry a contagious pathogen that can be passed to its innocent victims.

6: BEER-GOGGLE ZOMBIES

There is no greater testimony to the zombie's popularity than the spectacular overuse of the word in the last thirty years. *Zombie* has been used to refer to so many different kinds of entities and social dynamics that it is now hard to rein it in with any specificity. By one expert's account, for example, anyone who has died and been brought back to life is a zombie. This means that people who flatline on the operating table before being revived are doomed to be zombies for the rest of their lives.

Movie critics aren't any better at using *zombie* responsibly. One critic cited Johnny Depp as starring in the top-grossing zombie movie of all time, 2003's *Pirates of the Caribbean: The Curse of the Black Pearl.* The film raked in more than $650 million worldwide and has spawned a number of highly profitable sequels. The only problem is that *Pirates* clearly isn't a zombie movie, as any five-year-old who's seen it can tell you. There is not a single creature in it that remotely approximates a zombie in any way, shape, or form. Meaningless generalizations like this would make me want to pull my hair out, if only I had any.

What I like to call beer-goggle zombies are creatures that are not related to the modern zombie, but if you're really drunk and you can't fully form a logical train of thought, then you might be tempted to think they are zombies.

Apparently, zombie catalogers drink a lot. Here are some monsters that frequently appear in zombie film catalogs and zombie guides both online and in traditional print publications. A simple litmus test is applied to the creatures below to see how well they conform to the modern zombie's three-tiered definition.

FRANKENSTEIN

Litmus Test:
~~Relentlessly Aggressive~~
~~Reanimated Human Corpse~~
~~Biological Infection~~

It is often said that there is a long-standing debate between zombie enthusiasts about whether or not Frankenstein is a zombie. Not really. There's no debate that I'm aware of, at least not one between two sane people. Mary Shelley's monster is not a zombie.

Though Dr. Frankenstein uses scientific means to create his creature in Shelley's novel, he's not a reanimated corpse. In fact, he's not a corpse at all but a collection of body parts stolen from different corpses and brought together to form a single new entity. Frankenstein is also not a reanimated corpse in the sense of being undead. He has a heartbeat and is fully alive in the classical sense of being a living creature. He is brought to life rather than reanimated.

Frankenstein is furthermore not relentlessly aggressive. He's quite a sensitive and thoughtful guy. He even tries to learn how to read and desires, above all, to be loved. He's driven to anger and destructiveness through his mistreatment by humans, who discriminate against him largely because of his appearance.

Finally, the process by which he was made to exist does not involve an infection. He has no contagion to spread to others. In fact, he doesn't have a "condition" at all, except for the tragedy of his loneliness. Later Hollywood versions of Frankenstein make him less sympathetic and more predatory, but his essential problem remains: he just doesn't fit in with others.

Not a zombie.

MUMMIES

Litmus Test:
~~Relentlessly Aggressive~~
Reanimated Human Corpse
~~Biological Infection~~

Really? This one is pretty clear. It's even got its own name, *mummy*, illustrating the point that if a monster is actually identified as something else in particular, it's relatively safe to assume that it's not a zombie.

For the record, mummies are not zombies because they are not relentlessly aggressive and they do not come to be through a biological infection. A mummy is a corpse whose skin and organs have been preserved by either intentional or incidental exposure to chemicals, extreme coldness, low humidity, or some combination thereof. In ancient mummy lore, they often protect specific places or sacred items, and this is also their driving desire in Hollywood depictions.

Mummies are not revived through some scientific process but, rather, through the fulfillment of a curse or eternal mission. Once order is restored to the mummy's world—meaning once you give it back its favorite ruby brooch or leave its sacred space—it will lie down again and wait for the next time someone disturbs its rest.

Mummies may be creepy and cool, but they are not related to zombies in the least.

DEMONS

Litmus Test:
~~Relentlessly Aggressive~~
Reanimated Human Corpse
~~Biological Infection~~

Like mummies, demons also have their own label, which suggests right away that they're not zombies. What separates dramatic depictions of demons from those of the modern zombie is that demon aggression is a matter of choice and is often specifically targeted to a limited number of individuals.

Demons are also driven by supernatural possession, not biological infection. A demon enters the body of its choosing, either living or dead, and asserts its will on that body to its own ends. Demonic possession isn't contagious, although it's difficult to overcome. But once the evil spirit leaves the possessed body it is returned to its natural state. There's really nothing here that relates to zombies.

Nevertheless, some filmmakers and critics have tried to tie them together. Sam Raimi's 1981 romp, *The Evil Dead,* is the classic example of a demonic movie often mistaken to be a zombie movie. In it, demons are accidentally awakened in the woods surrounding an isolated cabin. They set about tormenting the film's lead, Bruce Campbell, and picking off his friends one by one.

Though human corpses do stand up, dance about, and attack the living, the demonic force behind their actions also causes trees and plants to come alive; turns slight young women into flying, bug-eyed maniacs with superhuman strength; and makes windows and doors swing about wildly as if the demon is possessing the entire building. When's the last time you saw a real zombie do that?

Evil Dead (1981)

ASH: Did something in the woods do this to you?

CHERYL: No, it was the woods themselves! They're alive, Ash! They're alive.

LINDA: Ash, why don't I take her in the back room so she can lie down.

CHERYL: I'm not lying down! I want to get out of here. I want to leave this place right now!

JESUS OF NAZARETH

Litmus Test:
~~Relentlessly Aggressive~~
~~Reanimated Human Corpse~~
~~Biological Infection~~

OK, according to Christian belief, Jesus did rise from the dead. But by all accounts, he was just as much himself after coming back from the dead as he was before his crucifixion. Zombies, on the other hand, share nothing in common with the human who once occupied their bodies, except for the physical body itself. Technically speaking, a zombie is not a person raised from the dead but, rather, a new creature animating the shell of what was once a living human being. The former person is gone, and something new has taken his or her place. Also, Jesus ascends to heaven after being resurrected, while zombies aren't going anywhere. The verdict on Jesus? Not a zombie. Although the biblical prophet Zechariah does seem to prophesy a zombie pandemic, which ought to give us all something to think about:

> *The Lord will send a plague to all the nations that fought Jerusalem. Their flesh will rot where they stand, their eyes will rot in their sockets, and their tongues will rot in their mouths. The people will be stricken by a great panic, and they will attack one another.* (14:12–13)

In the meantime, Jesus's not-zombieness is helpful in illustrating a core quality of zombies: they aren't the person whose body they occupy. Think of the body as a house and the zombie as a squatter. The rightful owners have moved on, and someone else has taken up residence in what should be an abandoned property. So if you ever have the misfortune of running into a recently deceased family member shambling up your driveway with a hunger for human flesh, don't hesitate to take swift and violent action. That's not Uncle Bob anymore; that's just some freeloader wearing his skin and bones.

KNOW YOUR ZOMBIES: COLONEL HERZOG

Dead Snow (2009)

Colonel Herzog and his undead Nazi troops behave much like mummies—they are preserved in ice, they just want their gold back, and they may not be contagious—but they're called zombies by name throughout *Dead Snow*, making the intentions of this Norwegian romp clear.

Earlier Nazi zombie movies include *Shock Waves* (1977) and *Zombie Lake* (1981), both of which involve ghouls rising from bodies of water to terrorize the living.

ILLUSTRATION BY WILLIAM BLANKENSHIP

SECTION II

ZOMBIE SCIENCE

I went to a demolition derby several years back, and it struck me that the competing cars had a lot in common with zombies. If you've never seen it, demolition derby is a motorsport consisting of a number of similar cars competitively ramming into one another until only one is still operational, while the rest lie motionless and destroyed.

Cars prepped for a derby are stripped down to their bare essentials. The lights are removed, the seats are ripped out, the suspension is cut down to a minimum, the dashboard is  stripped, and the radio is trashed. Anything that doesn't directly assist in the accomplishment of the driver's narrow objective is history. Just like a zombie occupying what was once a fully functioning human body, the derby car is a shell of its former self.

A derby car isn't tasked with having a long and productive driving life. Its only goal is to survive the other cars on the track for at least a few brief seconds. Zombies are likewise designed not for longevity but, rather, for viability. They only need to live long enough to spread their infection to a new host.

There's a lot we can't know about zombie physiology until the dead come clawing back for us. But examining the complex inner workings of a zombie through the lens of something as simple as a demolition derby may help to clarify the potential issues at hand. I know it does for me.

Re-Animator (1985)

DR. HILL: I want your discovery. Whatever it is that gives the dead the appearance of life.

WEST: It is not the appearance of life, it is life. This is not magic. I am a scientist.

DR. HILL: I'll have you locked up as a madman or a murderer!

The scientific community has embraced the living dead as a legitimate field of study in recent years. Largely because of their uniquely biological roots, zombies are the perfect research subjects, and serious work is being done in a wide range of fields, from mathematical outbreak modeling to the theoretical construction of the zombie brain.

In their paper "When Zombies Attack: Mathematical Modeling of an Outbreak of Zombie Infection," a University of Ottawa research team concluded that a large-scale zombie outbreak would lead to societal collapse unless dealt with quickly and aggressively. The *New York Times* included the work among its top ideas of 2009.

That same year, Dr. Steven Schlozman, codirector of medical student education in psychiatry at Harvard Medical School, gained national attention for his theory of ataxic neurodegenerative satiety deficiency syndrome (ANSD), which seeks to explain classic zombie behaviors such as slight uncoordination, reduced brain function, and perpetual hunger and aggression. Schlozman fictionalized the syndrome in his 2011 novel, *The Zombie Autopsies.* As he says:

In my novel, ANSD is the name given to the condition of zombie-ism by the World Health Organization. It is an airborne bug, spread in respiratory droplets like the common cold; though being bitten by someone with ANSD is a potent vector of disease transmission as well.

Let me be clear, though: all zombie research is theoretical. We don't have an available walking corpse to capture, strap down, and cut up for the good of mankind, so certain assumptions need to be made on an individual basis. Though zombies are classified as dead, Schlozman's theory is that they have beating hearts and that their lungs continue to take in oxygen. Other theories are built around flesh eaters that don't breathe at all. Likewise, the Ottawa researchers also used their own specific set of parameters when developing their model.

No single theory will ever paint a complete picture of the modern zombie, and we'll never know the full extent of the threat we face until the dead rise. But by taking a close look at the most compelling new and developing research in the field, we might foster a better understanding of the coming threat, thereby increasing our chance of survival as a species.

To that end, this section looks at the theoretical biology of the modern zombie, establishes its defining behavioral characteristics, and identifies existing pathogens that could be possible infection sources. We will also highlight strange zombielike animals from around the world and touch on disturbing current events that seem to suggest that all signs point to the coming plague.

7: THE ZOMBIE BRAIN

 In 2007, I attended *Wired* magazine's fourth annual Nextfest in Los Angeles, a showcase of technological innovations meant to change the world. The convention featured dozens of exhibits, including a giant holographic fighting game, a single-wheeled motorcycle concept, and a gaggle of yellow dancing marshmallow balls. But the one demonstration that everyone wanted to see, billed by organizers as the premier spectacle of the entire show, was Kiyomori the samurai robot. So special was Kiyomori that it only came out of its fancy samurai battle tent twice a day.

Thirty minutes before Kiyomori's scheduled appearance, crowds began to form along the rope, so I found a spot near the front and dug in to witness the future of robotics. My head swirled with visions of a fierce fighting machine that jumped and kicked and expertly readied its samurai sword for battle. What was about to happen? Would Kiyomori go haywire and kill an innocent bystander before wreaking havoc on the entire city? I'd seen *Robocop*; I knew the risks. Was this mysterious metal samurai a fateful precursor to Ed-209 or T-800? Maybe I should have sat farther back.

Ominous Japanese music started, Kiyomori's introduction was made over a loudspeaker, and then it appeared. The robot hobbled forward on shaky legs, slowly moving to a fixed position in the small ring. Far from an intimidating warrior, it looked like a tin suitcase with legs and arms in a cheap Halloween costume. Two nervous handlers stood on either side of Kiyomori, making sure it didn't fall over. Needless to say, it was less than impressive to a robotics novice like me but paradoxically also not overbilled. Kiyomori *was* the future.

In March 2009, Japan's National Institute of Advanced Industrial Science and Technology debuted its new female humanoid robot at Tokyo Fashion Week. The Center for Advanced Vehicles at the University of Tehran, Iran, followed suit in August 2010 with a shiny white biped called Surena 2. Neither is substantially more physically capable than Kiyomori.

Thousands of the brightest minds on the planet have spent decades tackling this problem but have yet to create a life-sized humanoid robot that can move through space as well as even the most awkward zombie.[14] The robots can't avoid rotting bodies in the road or navigate cracked curbsides or burned-out porch stairs. They can't maintain balance while grabbing, pulling, and eating their struggling victims alive. They can't kneel to feast on the flesh of their fallen prey. What they can do is walk in a straight line on a smooth surface and then turn around and walk back again.

This isn't a knock on robotics but, rather, the most striking evidence that the walking dead are more capable and likely smarter than most give them credit for. There is an inexorable connection between the brain and the body, so through theoretical observation of zombie behavior, we know that the zombie brain must be relatively high-functioning. Maybe not high-functioning compared to your average human, but certainly high-functioning compared to Kiyomori.

Put another way, your undead neighbor may not be likely to take up poetry as a hobby or memorize all the provinces of

Canada. But the very fact that he's able to recognize a door or a window, claw at it to gain entry, then identify, chase, and capture food across wide swaths of varying terrain is a testament to his impressive undead brainpower.

STRUCTURE AND FUNCTION

Timothy Verstynen, PhD, is a neuroscientist at the Center for the Neural Basis of Cognition in Pittsburgh, specializing in human brain imaging and neural network modeling. Bradley Voytek, PhD, is a neuroscientist at the University of California, Berkeley, studying the role of neural oscillations in communicating brain networks. Together they authored a groundbreaking paper on zombie brain function titled "The Living Dead Brain," in connection with their development of a complete three-dimensional model of a zombie brain. To say that these guys know what they're talking about when it comes to the structure and function of the zombie brain is an understatement.

Voytek and Verstynen pioneered the theory of Consciousness Deficit Hypoactivity Disorder in the undead, defined as the loss of rational, voluntary, and conscious behavior, replaced by delusional, impulsive aggression; stimulus-driven attention; and the inability to coordinate motor and linguistic behaviors. In other words, zombies aren't the most graceful creatures on the planet, but they sure do want to rip your guts out:

Together, these symptoms and their neurological roots reveal a striking picture of the zombie brain. Based on the behavioral profile of the standard zombie, we conclude that the zombie brain would have massive atrophy of the "association areas" of the brain: those areas that are responsible for the higher-order cognitive functions. Given the clear cognitive and memory deficits, we would also expect significant portions of the frontal and parietal lobes, and nearly the entire temporal lobe, to exhibit massive degeneration.[15]

Echoing their work, McGill University researchers offer a clear breakdown of the human brain's control over motor function, explaining that even basic movements—walking, looking around, grabbing—require complementary actions taken by the brain as a whole. It's akin to a ship's crew, whereby the frontal lobe receives information about the individual's current position from several other parts, then, like the ship's captain, issues commands. The major difference between humans and zombies is that commands such as *Walk to your car to go to work* or *Open the microwave to heat up a Hot Pocket* are changed to *Eat Mr. Johnson mowing his lawn* and *Eat the paramedic helping Mr. Johnson.*

CAN ZOMBIES LEARN?

A 2010 study at Carnegie Mellon University showed that humans and other animals use real and hypothetical memory to help make basic decisions. When applied to zombie research, this fact suggests that the undead probably have some developmental ability in order to hunt their human prey effectively. In layman's terms, zombies might learn.

The study found that rats navigating a maze used not only replays of recent or frequent paths through the maze but also paths that they'd rarely taken or had not yet taken at all. The rats were trying to build mental maps to help them make navigation choices, proving that memory is an integral part of the decision-making process. Researcher Anoopum Gupta notes that this is true even if the goal is something as simple as sniffing out a piece of cheese:

> *Our work provides clues into how animals must construct a complete, fully navigable representation of their environment in order to move around, even if they've only partially explored that environment.*[16]

Memory and learning are so tied to our ability to make simple choices that without them, a zombie would likely not be able to tell the difference between a door and a wall, let alone find its way out of a dead-end alley. A front door covered in paper or tape could be enough to confuse this type of zombie, rendering the door virtually invisible.

But to understand the potential differences between learning in the living and in the undead, we look to findings from the California Institute of Technology that show that humans use a complex combination of two learning processes to navigate through their world: (1) model-free learning and (2) model-based learning.

Model-free learning is based on trial-and-error comparisons between the anticipated reward and the reward we actually receive in any given situation. For example, a zombie bangs its head against a brick wall and doesn't gain access to the screaming children inside the house. It then bangs its head against a window, the window breaks, and the zombie gets rewarded with a nice meal. Moving forward it will now be more interested in windows than walls.

By contrast, model-based learning is a more complex system whereby the brain builds a virtual map of the environment to understand different situations. A model-based thinker doesn't need to stick with what he knows from past experience and so is able to make sudden strategic shifts.

If zombies are indeed unable to accomplish complex tasks such as unlocking doors or using weapons, it may be because they rely too heavily on a largely model-free view of the world that is not adequately balanced by the higher-functioning model-based system. In this case, they could learn little lessons along the way, such as that walls aren't good for eating children but windows are. They would not, however, achieve great leaps in knowledge and eventually overpower humans with their smarts alone.

According to Romero, zombies develop the ability to work together in teams. They communicate with one another. They can learn to enjoy music, follow directions, use weapons, and eventually even outsmart humans. Romero zombies also retain memory of their past lives and personalities and act out past rituals and habits. Their learning ability seems to far outpace common beliefs about the modern zombie.

Zombies apparently must possess some level of memory and learning to navigate through our world, and the limit to their developmental abilities may be related to their sleeping habits. A study from Harvard University strongly suggests that sleep enhances memory and learning in humans. If, as many believe, the undead never actually rest in their constant search for fresh meat, a zombie's inability to develop new skills may have much more to do with its insomnia than with its actual potential to learn.

The Harvard study's coauthor Robert Stickgold explains that task-related dreams are triggered by the sleeping brain's desire to consolidate challenging new information and to figure out how to use it. Making even the most basic choices requires constant low-level learning, but if zombies don't sleep at all, then their ability to collect data and cognitively advance may be shot.

By endlessly hunting humans, the undead may be robbing themselves of the chance to become even deadlier hunters.

So if you ever see a zombie nodding off for a quick nap, you might want to think about waking it up.

A sleeping zombie could be a learning zombie, and nobody wants that.

Land of the Dead (2005)

RILEY: They're moving toward the city.

KAUFMAN: They'll never get across the river.

RILEY: I wouldn't be so sure. They're learning how to work together.

KAUFMAN: They're mindless walking corpses, and many of us will be too if you don't stay focused on the task at hand. Zombies, man. They creep me out.

KNOW YOUR ZOMBIES: BUB

Day of the Dead (1985)

Romero's third zombie film depicts the undead as capable of learning new skills and evolving over time. Bub still craves human flesh, but he's not such a bad guy overall. He enjoys music, has a basic understanding of tools, salutes his superior officers, and even learns how to shoot a pistol.

While Bub becomes more refined, the humans in *Day of the Dead* devolve into a chaotic, bickering gang of thugs. Romero begs the question: who is the real menace?

ILLUSTRATION BY JOSH TAYLOR

8: ZOMBIE BLOOD

Human blood is charged with delivering needed nutrients and oxygen to waiting cells in the body and removing waste from those same cells. It contains a substance called hemoglobin, which gives blood its color and contains enough iron to make red cells subject to the effects of magnetic fields.

Many cultures have used magnetic therapy to treat illness and encourage blood flow to specific parts of the body for centuries. A 2003 University of Virginia study showed that human blood can be propelled through the vascular system by magnets.

Because it's clear that the undead possess a fundamentally different physiology from that of your typical human corpse, as evidenced by their walking around and eating people, it may be that changes occurring in the electrical pulses of the brain as it passes from human to zombie create the necessary conditions for magnetization.

STAGNATION OR CIRCULATION?

Though it is widely believed that all blood flow in a person infected with the zombie sickness ceases at death, a compelling counterargument might be that the undead brain has a constant hunger for blood in order to continue working properly.

A brain without blood flow would very quickly dry out, crack, and become little more than a lump of brittle nothing. University of California, Berkeley, neuroscience professor Marian Diamond points out that without blood irrigation to the brain, all channels would flatten, and there would be no brain function and no sitting up or walking around. So it makes sense that there is a mechanism for zombie blood flow.

In a living human, 20 percent of the blood pumped from the heart goes into the brain. To put this in perspective, an adult male dedicates up to 500 percent more blood to his brain than should be required by weight distribution. Even if zombies function at a substantially reduced capacity compared with their human counterparts, the amount of blood used on a constant basis is staggering. So it stands to reason that if there is blood moving in the brain, then there should be blood moving through other parts of the body.

And if blood does move through zombie bodies without the aid of a beating heart, we must then discover what is likely driving the system and exactly how it works. As is often the case in zombie research, a single hypothesis leads to many more questions.

Because the pathogen moves freely throughout the host, is it possible that the pathogen itself has evolved an independent oxygen-carrying capability?
— The Zombie Autopsies (2011), Steven Schlozman

One thing is certain: it's impossible for the undead to present a credible threat to the living if their blood reacts in a similar manner to that of deceased humans, because they would simply not be able to move around well enough to hunt. The gravitational pooling of blood in a corpse, called livor mortis, causes blood to flow toward the part of the body closest to the ground. As the blood accumulates, that area swells and becomes discolored, stretching the flesh to the point of breakage.

In the case of a zombie that stands up and seeks out prey, livor mortis could mean that all blood inside the body quickly moves to the feet, bursting through the skin and destroying any remaining tissue. The undead menace would be literally walking on bones alone. And those bones, absent the protective casing of flesh and muscle, would also break apart in short order.

So unless you believe that zombies are short creatures that awkwardly hobble around on leg-bone stumps, more prone to falling over than to eating people, it seems clear that something is happening to undead blood to make it behave differently from how it normally would in a corpse.

SPREADING THE INFECTION

The zombie sickness is generally believed to be spread through the transfer of blood, saliva, or other bodily fluids. You get bitten or sprayed in the mouth and eyes with toxic zombie goo, and soon enough, you're weak, confused, and fast on the road to becoming an undead ghoul yourself. Because of this, Todd Thorne, president of the International Association of Blood Pattern Analysts, argues that zombie blood must circulate, even without being forcibly pumped by a beating heart, or else it wouldn't be able to transmit from one body to another. In fact, without circulation, there would be no blood at all.

Blood-borne illnesses travel through the human body by catching a free ride on our fast-moving highway of arteries and veins, but after death, the highway grinds to a sudden halt. If zombie blood doesn't flow on its own, then the infection would stop advancing at the moment a person dies. In the case of a quick death, the tainted blood wouldn't have time to reach the brain or central nervous system, and that newly dead person would therefore not become a zombie.

Following this logic, if zombified blood is not able to flow at will, then a person who is bitten on the hand and soon after fatally shot through the chest would likely not become a zombie even though the brain was never destroyed. As long as death occurs before the zombie infection has fully taken hold, then another member of the undead legion would not be created.

ROMERO'S RULES

In Romero's world, everyone who dies for any reason turns into a zombie. The zombie bite only serves to speed up a person's death but doesn't change the inevitable fate of every man, woman, and child on the planet to turn into a flesh starved zombie once expired. The cause of death is not important, as it is the death itself that creates the new zombie.

Adding more weight to the argument that zombie blood likely flows, in 2010, researchers at Vanderbilt University showed that when cells move about in humans, they mimic the behavior of amoebae and bacteria searching for food. Study participant Alka Potdar explains that for the first time, we have a general framework for fully understanding the way cells move. And since the framework for self-propelled motion already exists inside human beings, a zombie sickness has only to insert its own selfish intention into the body's existing structure to create an army of walking dead that enjoy the benefits of some level of blood flow.

Star Trek: Infestation #1 (2011)

MCCOY: Whatever was transmitted from Padilla's bite is coursing through your system with unprecedented speed and aggression.

BARNES: You mean it's going to happen to me too? You've got to do something!

KIRK: Bones, isn't there anything . . .

MCCOY: Damn it, Jim. I don't even know what we're dealing with yet!

And if zombie blood does in fact flow through the body in some manner, this may have an impact on the commonly held belief that the undead freeze in cold weather. A zombie with flowing blood probably functions much more like a cold-blooded animal than the warm-blooded human it used to be.

Several species of cold-blooded fish have a special substance in their blood called glycoprotein, which acts like antifreeze to help them survive very cold water temperatures. Glycoprotein depresses the freezing temperature of blood sufficiently to render the body immune to the cold. Much like a bottle of vodka in a freezer box, while everything around it is frozen stiff, it never changes from its liquid state.

If the undead body is able to access the existing glycoprotein therein, it may then have a workable system that no longer needs to regulate internal temperature in order to function. Though zombies would still likely move more slowly in extreme cold, their blood would never convert into a solid, continuing to flow and power the body.

9: ZOMBIE HUNTING TECHNIQUE

Though he never made a zombie movie, Alfred Hitchcock is one of the pioneering masters of modern horror in film. Reflecting on what causes people to feel the chill of fear right down to their very bones, Hitchcock observed that there is no terror in the bang, only in the anticipation of it. And isn't that the true essence of the zombie?

In their pure relentlessness, zombies are consummate hunters. They are the embodiment of a constant awareness of the inevitability of death. They never stop. They never plot or scheme. They can't be bargained with or shown sense in reason. They have no meaning, no choice, not even any recognition of the existence of choice. They're simply forever shambling your way, hunting you, trying to get just close enough to claw, to grasp, to chew.

They have no regard for the survival of any species, including their own. As long as they're able, zombies will hunt until every last available prey is either destroyed or turned into yet another undead ghoul. *Sustainable living* isn't in a flesh eater's vocabulary, and this spells big trouble for the human race. But could their insatiable appetite actually be the magic bullet that saves the planet?

Mass extinction of species throughout history has served as Mother Nature's reset button, periodically allowing the earth to refresh and renew itself. However, many scientists argue that humans are unnaturally speeding up this process through overpopulation, resource depletion, and climate change, ultimately leading to irreparable damage. Cue the zombies.

In the event of a global zombie plague, there would be no need for a new ice age to destroy the billions of different animals and plants already living in harmony. Mankind, as the infecting parasite that has upset this delicate balance, would simply eat itself out of the equation. As the remaining hordes eventually sank back into the earth, the rest of the world's species would then be able to go on living as if we were never here in the first place.

It's great fun to crash a bus through a department store window as the driver finds himself torn to shreds by the suddenly zombified passengers. But in the end the world, appearance-wise, survives.
—Zombie Spaceship Wasteland *(2011), Patton Oswalt*

Of course, the fact that your demise may contribute to the global good will likely provide little comfort when a pack of hungry zombies breaks through your hasty home defenses to chew your arms off. If any of us hopes to survive long enough to see us destroy the planet ourselves, a more complete understanding of how the undead may hunt the living is needed.

HOW DO THEY FIND US?

Prevailing wisdom suggests that zombies do not simply stumble about without purpose but, instead, do everything in their power to relentlessly hunt and kill the living. To that end, their seemingly random pattern of movement when not actively

stalking prey may more closely mirror that of many predators when locating food over great distances.

Hungry sharks, turtles, fish, and other marine predators use a hunting system known as the Levy walk or Levy flight.[17] Though it appears to be random wandering, the Levy walk is actually a superior strategy for finding prey in vast areas where food is sparse and hidden.

David Sims of Britain's Marine Biological Association developed a computer model confirming that the predatory patterns are optimal for naturally dynamic prey fields, because the Levy walk involves moving in short bursts in many different directions, before taking a long advance toward a single point and then repeating the process. This allows a hunter to investigate one location before jumping to a completely different spot.

A 2010 study done by researchers at North Carolina State University found that humans also follow the Levy-walk patterns commonly observed in animals such as monkeys and birds:

Our study is based on about one thousand hours of GPS traces involving 44 volunteers in various outdoor settings including two different college campuses, a metropolitan area, a theme park and a state fair.[18]

If zombies instinctually employ the Levy walk the way sharks and humans do, their travels around a mostly abandoned city would allow them the best chance of finding and eating the few remaining humans left. In rural areas, a remote farmhouse could be stumbled upon in the least amount of time and with less effort, meaning that the apparently chaotic movement of the undead may in fact be leading them straight to your front door.

Hell of the Living Dead (1981)

MAN: I can't see how many of them there are.

WOMAN: Just look at their faces. They look like monsters.

MAN: They could be drunk, or drugged. Or maybe it's a leper colony. They probably don't intend us any harm.

WOMAN: I don't know. I wouldn't be too sure.

ZOMBIE TOUCH

Once a zombie is within striking distance of its potential meal, how is it able to differentiate its living prey from others of its own kind? If zombies hunt by sight, then walking like a zombie could afford potential victims functional invisibility. If they hunt by smell, then certain antiodor measures could be employed. Looking at the hunting technique of the smallest predatory mammal on the planet, the Etruscan shrew, one interesting hypothesis suggests that zombies use their sense of touch to find, capture, and devour their victims.

The tiny shrew must eat twice its body weight every day to keep from starving, and the animals it hunts—crickets, cockroaches, and spiders—are often as big as the shrew itself. It spots potential prey visually, then moves in to feel and confirm. Much like a zombie reaching out for its next meal, the shrew decides what to attack by touching targets with its nose and whiskers.

Because it's widely believed that zombies are cold-blooded and because their imperfect body is dead and rotting, it stands to reason that the undead would have no trouble identifying a warm, soft, living person using this touch method. Interestingly, this may also explain why zombies are thought to move about in packs. If they gather to investigate one another through touch, they would then be in a naturally formed group as they moved on to seek out humans to eat.

ZOMBIE SMELL

Another notion of zombie hunting behavior made popular in part by the hit AMC television series *The Walking Dead* is that zombies identify the living primarily through sense of smell. Though they are rotting corpses and therefore likely give off the revolting scent of death, the undead's olfactory abilities may be enhanced through the same process that is a common side effect observed in users of psychedelic drugs.

Hyperosmia is a condition in humans that causes an acute increase in the ability to smell. It is often seen in patients with cluster headaches or migraines, but tests have shown that recreational use of LSD can result in the same or a similar outcome. Because it's generally accepted that zombies are driven by their brains, it stands to reason that a brain disorder affording the living a tremendous increase in their sense of smell may also be at work in the undead.

> *The other corpse had already awakened next to it. Its face twitched up and down as if sniffing her through whatever remained of its nose.*
> —Star Wars: Death Troopers *(2009), Joe Schreiber*

People suffering from Addison's disease, wherein the adrenal glands produce insufficient steroid hormones, are also inclined to experience hyperosmia. Zombies are unlikely to be producing steroids with their limited body functions, so a de facto Addison's hyperosmia scenario could be at work.

THE PACK MENTALITY

The modern zombie is nothing if not relentlessly aggressive, but the second-most universally espoused belief about undead behavior is that zombies generally move in large packs, or hordes. However, they are also thought not to work together when seeking out and attacking prey. This seeming contradiction could be explained away by their hunting style, or it could be a function of something more innate within the zombie's core being.

When it comes to the zombie horde, could a more developed social structure be at work? Honeybees, along with ants and wasps, are able to carry out complex tasks involving thousands of individual participants with little or no communication. They all do their own thing, completely unaware of what their fellow bees are up to, but still they present a unified front, each marching toward a single goal.

Furthermore, the aggressive behavior created by the hive mind of bees is extremely similar to a typical depiction of a zombie outbreak. A horde of zombies may not work together or communicate in any traditional sense, but at the same time, they really represent a formidable threat only when they present a unified front, attacking as a group.

A colony of bees is often described by experts as being functionally one creature. Each bee is just a part of a single entity. Looking at the undead in a similar way would help to explain why they possess such a complete disregard for their individual well-being. The destruction of one particular zombie is meaningless to the horde, as long as they continue moving forward toward the ultimate objective of devouring the entire human race.

Ants use this same method of universal mind, and they also hunt primarily through sense of touch and smell, as suggested in the previous section.

DO ZOMBIES MOAN?

Pick a zombie movie made in the past fifty years, and chances are you'll hear at least a few of the ghouls moaning up a storm. Very scary on the big screen, but are real zombies actually able and willing to make primitive utterances? Research out of the University of Massachusetts, Amherst, suggests that they're likely silent, and it all boils down to the meaning behind a dog's bark.

The extensive 2009 study concluded that barking in dogs is associated with a clearly definable behavior known as mobbing, a cooperative antipredator response. By contrast, wild animals normally have plenty of room to move, so when they hear something, they silently run away or run toward the source of the noise. But even in the wild, animals that can't flee or attack will bark, head researcher Kathryn Lord explains:

> Even birds bark, and certainly many mammals besides canines, including baboons and monkeys, rodents and deer also bark. In a whole bunch of mammals and birds, what they do in conflicted situations is bark.[19]

They bark as a warning to a perceived threat to leave the area and as an alert to other potential prey that danger is near. But because zombies are thought to be single-minded predators with no defensive instinct at all and because it's widely held that zombies don't hunt in coordinated teams, the argument for a moaning zombie has some clear logical flaws.

If they're not trying to ward off a threat or alert their partners, why would they bother making any sound at all? Noise only serves to reveal their position and makes their objective harder to obtain. Don't get me wrong, I hope zombies moan. I hope they play instruments and march down Main Street like a Thanksgiving Day band so we can all hear them coming from blocks away. Unfortunately, that just might not be the case.

Bucking later popular trends once again, Romero's flesh eaters are silent. In some of his films, such as *Land of the Dead*, they do display very limited vocalization, making utterances only when directly communicating with other zombies. They never engage in prolonged bouts of moaning for seemingly no reason and often sneak up on unsuspecting victims because they are so quiet.

ROMERO'S RULES

In her bestselling book *Animals in Translation*, Temple Grandin explains that attacks meant to kill for the purpose of feeding are nothing like the growling, loud encounters that animals have when trying to protect themselves or their territory. Extensive observation has proven that a killer on the hunt is almost always quiet and expressionless. In fact, animal behaviorists commonly refer to predatory killing as the "quiet bite."

This evidence reinforces the argument that zombies likely don't moan. Grandin states clearly that animals on the hunt have no strategic reason to make any sound. In fact, noise puts them at a marked disadvantage and so is avoided at any cost.

So remember, just because the zombie at your front door isn't moaning and growling doesn't mean it's not interested in eating you alive. On the contrary, it may be more focused on that than even the most realistic Hollywood ghoul.

Night of the Living Dead (1968)

BEN: You mean you didn't hear the racket we were making up here?

HARRY: How were we supposed to know what was going on? Could have been those things for all we knew.

BEN: That girl was screaming. Surely you must know what a girl screaming sounds like. Those things don't make any noise!

10: DEFENSIVE REFLEX IN ZOMBIES

The 2008 film *Pontypool* follows the crew of a small morning radio show as reports of random violence and riots begin pouring in from callers in the usually sleepy surrounding town. It soon becomes clear that citizens are being turned from innocent victims to raving maniacs that will stop at nothing to attack and kill those unaffected.

Before long, the host and his producer are locked inside the sealed radio booth as their infected assistant outside slams her head repeatedly into the thick soundproof glass until her face is little more than a shattered mass of broken bones and swollen flesh. She wants what she wants, and she'll stop at nothing to get it. Though the film takes artistic license with the new breed of living-zombie story, *Pontypool*'s infected largely remain true to the relentless nature of the modern zombie in that they display pure unchecked aggression. They attack with no sense of consequence or concern for counterattack or injury.

Zombie defensive strategy is unique to all other species, both real and imagined, in that they have none. Why are the undead hordes forever on attack? What makes them show no concern for self-preservation? And how do they process pain?

CAN ZOMBIES FEEL PAIN?

It's widely believed that if you take a swing at a zombie with the business end of a shovel, it will not duck out of the way. Because of this, some mistakenly conclude that zombies don't have any physical sensations whatsoever, going as far as to say that this lack of feeling is a physical advantage over normal humans.

In reality, a zombie with no physical sensation would be unable to move. Far from terrifying, this creature could do little more than lie on the ground and bite in your general direction. Neuroscientist Bradley Voytek echoes this sentiment, stating conclusively that one key element in a zombie's ability to walk is the ability to feel the ground beneath one's feet.

However, it has been suggested that neuropathy, a disorder commonly associated with advanced diabetes that results in nerve damage and impaired sensation, can explain how zombies may be able to stalk humans without having any physical sensation. But Tina Tockarshewsky, executive director of the Neuropathy Association, refutes this argument, explaining that neuropathy causes numbness and pain in the hands and feet, creating a loss of sensation comparable to the feeling of wearing thin socks or gloves. It doesn't eliminate sensation or pain.

As neuropathy progresses, it results in reduced, or altered, sensation in the arms and legs. This is different from no feeling at all. If left untreated patients could eventually lose sensation altogether and be rendered unable to walk and confined to a wheelchair.

Though a zombie set on fire may not react to bodily injury, the fact remains that physical sensation must be present for it to grab, clutch, claw, tackle, chase, chew, bite, and effectively hunt the living. However, it is reasonable to suggest that zombies may not feel pain.

People with a rare nervous system disorder known as congenital insensitivity to pain with anhidrosis (CIPA) have no ability to sense pain, but they are able to feel pressure. Therefore, CIPA patients can navigate the world just as any other person does—they walk, run, play—but in doing so, they risk serious injury to themselves without even knowing.

CIPA sufferers often experience burns, broken limbs, and other self-inflicted wounds because their defensive reflex is largely shut off. Even though they can feel a knife going through their hand, it doesn't hurt, so why avoid it?

In humans, CIPA can prove to be an extremely damaging condition. Teething infants chew their tongues and lips to bloody shreds. Toddlers play too rough and hurt themselves and others. Teens act even more recklessly than their peers, and the problems often get worse with age. By contrast, in a zombie, this same trait would allow them to go to any length to accomplish their morbid objective.

Dead Set (2008)

VERONICA: Just make sure you pin his head down and cover his teeth.

JOPLIN: What if he gets loose?

VERONICA: Do it right and he won't.

JOPLIN: Yes, but what if he does?

VERONICA: Then he'll probably kill us!

WHAT DO ZOMBIES SEE?

Though it seems likely that zombies have at least diminished pain receptors, a clearer understanding of how visual information is processed by the brain may shed some light on their lack of involuntary responses, such as flinching and ducking. To that end, Rita Carter's work *The Human Brain Book* proves an invaluable resource. Carter explains that there are actually two types of vision present in humans:

> *Conscious vision is the familiar process of seeing and recognizing something, while unconscious vision uses information from the eyes to guide behavior without our knowledge of it happening.*[20]

Put another way, our conscious sight allows us to recognize the undead mailman as a zombie coming to eat us, and our unconscious sight helps us avoid the falling tree branch we didn't even realize we saw in the split second it comes crashing down.

Therefore, a lack of defensive posturing in the undead may be explained by a failure in its unconscious vision. Regardless of whether it can feel pain, understand a threat, or even desire to avoid physical damage, that zombie at your front door simply might not be able to see the bat in your hand before you connect with the side of its skull. This may especially be true if zombies' reaction times are greatly slowed, as is often theorized.

THE BEST DEFENSE IS A GOOD OFFENSE

Findings out of Italy suggest that the undead's lack of defensive behavior may have more to do with their hardwired strategy of coping with the threat they face than with their visual abilities.

In August 2010, researchers at the European Molecular Biology Laboratory discovered a switch in the human brain that controls fear, identifying the specific type of neuron that determines how animals react to frightening stimuli. When the switch is "up," a passive, fear-based response is triggered. When the switch is "down," aggression takes hold.

Study leader Cornelius Gross clarified the results, explaining that they were not blocking the actual fear but just changing the animals' responses to that fear. So in the case of zombies, their complete lack of defense, even when experiencing severe bodily injury, could simply mean that their fear switch is locked in the down position. The larger the perceived threat, the more violent and aggressive they become.

Still further research suggests that zombies may allow themselves to be freely injured as a selfless gesture that benefits their fellow ghouls. Evolutionary research conducted at Michigan State University's Beacon Center for the Study of Evolution in Action proved that populations of organisms that are physically or genetically similar act altruistically, thereby protecting the survival of the larger group. By that logic, it stands to reason that the reckless behavior of zombies could be a subconscious by-product of this same process.

Though it's generally believed that the undead don't technically work together in battle, any single zombie can function as the perfect decoy, sucking precious time, energy, and resources from a survivor, even as the initial attack fails. This ensures that future resistance will be weaker, thereby substantially increasing the odds that zombie number two, three, five, or ten will eventually succeed.

In the Michigan State model, regardless of the zombie body count, the final meal is always a steaming pile of fresh you.

11: ZOMBIE EATING HABITS

Ask anyone with even a casual knowledge of zombies what the undead eat, and more often than not, the response will be "Braiiiins!" But despite popular belief, the undead likely don't prefer your brain to any other part of your living body. In fact, the concept of a zombie craving brains is unique to the *Return of the Living Dead* film series, a semispoof collection of B-movies from the late 1980s and early 1990s. The flaw in this premise is revealed through simple physics.

Bite-compression work done by researchers from Rensselaer Polytechnic Institute, the United States' oldest technical university, found that the human mouth is both too flat and too weak to penetrate a human skull. Predators have long mouths that protrude outward to allow them to use their full force when biting down on their prey. The human mouth is inset and unable to open wide enough to get a good grip on anything larger than an apple.

Other less popular theories put forth in *Return of the Living Dead* include that burning zombies spreads infection; zombies can talk, think, and reason; zombies know how to use car radios; and any animal can become a zombie.

Return of the Living Dead Part II (1988)

JOEY: Come here, Brenda. Brenda!

BRENDA: Joey, you stay away from me.

JOEY: But your brains smell so good. They smell so rich and spicy.

BRENDA: Spicy? Joey, I am not into dead guys!

In fact, some research suggests that zombies may not eat anything at all but, rather, just bite and chew. Though seemingly simple, the act of swallowing is a complex neuromuscular activity controlled by several different parts of the brain. As it's commonly believed that the zombie brain is low-functioning compared to that of the average human, evidenced in part by lack of speech, swallowing may prove too complex a task for a zombie. Additionally, eating may be a death sentence.

Decomposition begins in the stomach, as bacteria feed on the soft tissue and organs. Pumping more soft tissue into the zombie gut could be like pouring gasoline on a flame. The rotting process might speed up, and the zombie would become a worthless pile of goo in no time flat. And even if zombies could swallow, they probably would not be able to digest what they ate. How often do you see a zombie stop for a bathroom break? That could lead to massive bloating, sluggishness, and loss of balance, as their midsections become stretched like heavy, rotten watermelons, further reducing their threat to able-bodied humans.

If zombies don't actually eat anything, is it possible that the undead may increase their longevity by literally eating themselves from the inside out? Many of the human body's internal organs, once vital to the survival of a living person, are not likely needed for a zombie to function. Because of this, the newly reanimated corpse has a portable store of food built right into its framework.

Humans can go weeks without food. But as they eventually reach the later stages of starvation, the body will literally eat itself. In fact, digestive-related organ failure is what usually kills a starved person. By contrast zombies may have no need for many of their organs. They would then be free to digest the heart, lungs, liver, and intestines without suffering any ill effects, thereby substantially increasing their life span.

Regardless of whether or not zombies actually swallow the human flesh they bite into, if they are able to digest their own organs, then the undead may be able to fend off harmful bacteria, while continuing to generate needed energy and extending their lives.

DO THEY EAT DEAD PEOPLE?

Do zombies eat dead people? The answer may seem obvious, as they are generally considered to be after one thing and one thing only: live flesh. Therefore, a zombie would pass right by an available dead body and continue hunting the living.

But imagine a group of zombies cornering you in a dead-end alley. You do everything you can to fight back, but eventually, their numbers are too great, and you are driven to the ground by clawing hands and gnashing teeth. The zombies chew on your fingers, rip off a leg, and make short work of your intestines. Soon enough, you die from the overwhelming pain and blood loss, which leads to another version of the same question.

At the moment your heart stops beating, do the zombies get up and wander off, or do they continue feasting on your lifeless corpse?

If you think they get up, then zombies don't eat dead people. But if you think they finish the job, sucking out your eyeballs and chewing on your forearm even after you've died, then zombies do at least eat the newly deceased. This may seem like a small point, but it could mean the difference between real hope for civilization's survival and total world collapse.

If zombies continue feeding on the dead, then they are effectively destroying their own reinforcements. A person with a deadly bite may rise up to become a zombie himself, but a body that has been chewed down to nothing won't be physically able to stand and search out new victims. Zombies could quite literally eat themselves out of existence.

My hope is that they have really big appetites and don't know when to say when.

DO THEY EAT ANIMALS?

It's often suggested that zombies bite human beings because they are driven to spread their disease to other viable hosts. Because, with rare exception, prevailing wisdom suggests that the zombie virus is likely only communicable to humans, it could be argued that the undead would therefore be drawn to human beings only and ignore all other living creatures.

But even if the zombie infection is only a threat to humans, it is also a generally accepted belief that zombies aren't the sharpest knives in the drawer, nor are they attacking the living because of some greater strategy. Zombies do what they do because they are driven to it and don't know how to do anything else. It's possible that a hunting zombie might not be able to differentiate between different species and therefore would essentially want to bite anything that moves.

ROMERO'S RULES

Romero's own rules on zombie eating habits have changed over time. In the original *Night of the Living Dead* (1968), the zombies eat anything alive, including bugs. But in *Survival of the Dead* (2009), a central plot concern is to train the zombies to eat something other than humans, and for the most part, they seem completely unwilling and uninterested.

But because zombies are thought not to work together and not to use any tools or weapons, it would be difficult for them to catch most animals in the wild even if they so desired.

An easy test for this is to go outside and attempt to catch a squirrel, mouse, or rat with your bare hands. Even a cat or a stray dog that doesn't want to be caught is going to be a nearly impossible goal, especially if you're not aided by any advance strategy or tools. So zombies may want to eat animals, but if their abilities are limited, as we suspect, then for the most part, it's just not going to work out for them.

Good news for your pet ferret Bobo, but you're still pretty much screwed.

KNOW YOUR ZOMBIES: TARMAN

Return of the Living Dead (1985)

Tarman crawls out of a fifty-gallon drum of toxic sludge with one thing on his mind: brains. A military experiment gone wrong, he is the first modern zombie to ever say "brains" and the first modern zombie to ever eat brains, making him one of the most iconic ghouls of all time.

William Stout, famed production designer of *Return of the Living Dead*, later worked on creature design for *Predator* (1987), *Men in Black* (1997), and *Pan's Labyrinth* (2006).

ILLUSTRATION BY WILLIAM STOUT

12: HOW LONG HAVE WE GOT?

We've all seen the unlucky saps in zombie movies who get bitten, fall ill, die soon after, and then come back as undead beasts themselves. But how exactly does the zombie sickness cause such a speedy death in its victims? Turns out your own immune system might do most of the work, acting as a final nail in your coffin.

Sepsis is a condition in which the body fights a severe infection that has spread via the bloodstream. The immune system goes into overdrive, overwhelming normal processes in the blood and leading to blood clots and organ failure. Patients who become septic must be quickly seen by medical professionals or risk falling into a state of shock. If they are left untreated, death can occur within a matter of hours.

More than 200,000 people die of sepsis each year in the United States alone, and the symptoms closely mirror those seen in depictions of the progression of the zombie sickness. If a flesh eater's bite can deliver enough toxic filth to induce septic shock, it doesn't need to be fatal, because your own immune system will react so violently to the invading sickness that you will essentially kill yourself. In fact, new findings suggest that a bite resulting in infection need not be as directly damaging as previously thought to be fatal.

A 2010 study of the causes of deadly inflammation at

Harvard Medical School found that when the cells in our body are damaged by injury, they release large quantities of mitochondrial DNA. Though harmless, the DNA debris is interpreted by our immune system to be foreign bacterial invaders, and legions of white blood cells are called into action, sometimes with fatal results.

Therefore, a microscopic zombie sickness could kill a newly infected person quickly without relying on any sophisticated mechanisms. It has only to launch small attacks on cells it doesn't need for future functions, thereby overwhelming the immune system and sending white blood cells into a deadly panic. Death by septic shock would quickly follow.

But to really address the question of how long we have, we must look at two factors: the incubation period of the zombie sickness and the zombie life span.

INCUBATION PERIOD

As the speed of zombies on the hunt has increased in recent years, so, it seems, has the rate of infection. Rather than a day or even several hours, films such as *28 Days Later* present a virus that takes full control of its host in just a matter of seconds. In the case of living zombies, the argument is that it can transform its victims much more quickly because there is no need to go through the traditional process of death and reanimation. But is that logic sound?

Dr. Natalie Mtumbo of the World Health Organization suggests that the living zombies are in many ways less realistic than their classic undead counterparts. She explains that a disease spreading instantly through the body goes against everything we know about the rules of pathology, and so the notion of an extended incubation period makes more sense, even if it includes death.[21]

Echoing this point, Dr. Phil Luton of the United Kingdom's Centre for Emergency Preparedness and Response asserts that infectious-disease transmission requires an incubation period during which the patient is asymptomatic:

> *It has to get into the body. Next it has to take over the body and reproduce itself. It then has to get out of the body again and spread to the next person. Normally for that process to happen would be a minimum of two to three days.*[22]

In 2005, the United States Centers for Disease Control and Prevention set up a network of training institutes across the country designed to strengthen the nation's readiness for catastrophic public-health disasters. On condition of anonymity, a senior researcher at one such facility discussed several zombie doomsday scenarios, noting that the impact of infectious disease comes down to four measurable factors: susceptibility, exposure, infection, and recovery (or death), known as the SEIR model.

Assuming that the entire world is susceptible to the sickness, the researcher said that if zombieism is spread through a bite or some other close bodily contact, then you have a potential exposure problem, and the faster the infection spreads, the less likely it is to affect a large population.

He concludes that a lightning-quick virus is not only scientifically unrealistic, but it would draw too much attention to those infected in the early stages ever to represent a serious global threat. Instead, a zombie virus would likely need to have a long latency period, allowing it to infect a wide range of people across the planet before any symptoms appeared.

Unless the zombie sickness has a long latency period, experts agree that although off the charts in terms of creepiness, it would be considerably less concerning from a public-health standpoint than existing airborne pathogens that can spread easily across great distances.

If it takes a longer time for human beings to die and turn into flesh-eating ghouls, then it is also possible for them to travel a farther distance from the original point of infection while still human.
   —Theories of International Politics and Zombies *(2011)*,
                                        Daniel W. Drezner

MOSQUITOES

If the infection does incubate more slowly and methodically, then there could be a troubling scenario at play with regard to its spread. Many blood-borne illnesses are transferred by mosquitoes. Malaria, for example, is almost exclusively passed from one carrier to another in this manner. But mosquitoes do not feed on dead animals or people, suggesting that zombies would not be part of their diet.

Mosquitoes use various cues to find food, but above all, they are olfactory creatures. Breath and body vapors draw them to their animal hosts, as does body temperature.[23] Therefore, it stands to reason that a cold, rotting zombie would look nothing like a warm, living, breathing human to a mosquito.

However, a newly infected person who is still alive and kicking may be able to spread the infection before he even shows any signs of being sick. If that were the case, and if the zombie incubation period is as long as days or weeks, then entire populations could be infected before anyone even knows there's a problem.

Even once a person realizes that he's sick, a real danger exists that the infection will be hidden from other survivors. Most zombie movies feature at least one infected character who hides his worsening condition from the rest of the group. He gets bitten on the arm and then simply puts a long-sleeved shirt on, pretending nothing ever happened. Filmmakers use this device to heighten drama and drive action, but in a real zombie outbreak, failure to identify and isolate the sick could mean certain death. And you can bet many infected won't be eager to announce their new death sentence to the world.

THE ZOMBIE LIFE SPAN

The zombie life span is a key element of survival research, because if an accurate timeline can be established, starting with reanimation and ending with the final stages of decomposition, then strategies and expectations can be adjusted accordingly, resulting in millions of lives saved.

First, it's important to note that by human physiological standards, zombies are dead. They are believed to have no heartbeat, their blood is cold, and their tissue is in a state of decay. So it stands to reason that by looking at the specifics of human decomposition, we can come closer to the truth about how long the modern zombie can function before rotting back into the earth.

The human corpse goes through several distinct stages of decay, including fresh, bloat, and putrefaction. In her 2004 *New York Times* bestseller, *Stiff*, Mary Roach clearly breaks down this progression, noting that a hallmark of fresh-stage decay is a process called autolysis, or self-digestion. Roach goes on to explain that all of the body's internal organs liquefy in the fresh stage, including the brain.

In fact, because the brain is so soft and so close to hungry bacteria in the mouth, it is one of the first organs to go. By the second stage of decomposition, bloat, the brain has already been turned into a worthless puddle of mush, unable to keep from leaking out of the nasal cavity, much less control the actions of a bloodthirsty zombie. Therefore, it seems likely that a zombie's life span lasts as long as the fresh stage of decomposition and not one moment longer.

Dr. Peter Cummings is a forensic pathologist and medical examiner at the Massachusetts Office of the Chief Medical Examiner and author of *The Neuropathology of Zombies*. His research suggests that the rate of decay could be significantly slowed in the undead, resulting in a life span that doesn't last weeks or months but years or even decades:

I think they may be rotting at a much slower pace, like the foot of a diabetic. Their feet rot and toes fall off, but it happens over time. I also think that by having some basic metabolism, and some electrical stimulation to the muscles, they can decompose much slower.

If the undead do rot at a much slower pace than their human counterparts, zombie blood itself could act as a preservative. Embalming fluid makes the body's cellular proteins toxic, so they can't act as a nutrient source for invading bacteria. If the body fluids in a zombie are toxic, as is widely believed, it is possible that the system acts in a similar fashion to embalming fluid, thus slowing down decomposition considerably.

No matter what the process, it's highly unlikely that zombies survive indefinitely. If nothing else, exposure to the elements over time would break down the undead body from the outside in. Flesh would eventually wear away, and bone would become brittle and prone to breakage.

But if zombies don't decay from the inside out as dead humans do, if they are not susceptible to the same hungry bacteria that turn our dead organs into mush in just a matter of days, then the critical window of survival may be much longer than anyone previously thought.

ZOMBIE SLEEP

A 2009 sleep experiment from the University of Chicago proved that after thirty days of total sleep deprivation, a seemingly healthy rat will drop dead. In fact, all complex animated creatures—humans, rats, sheep, cockroaches—need some form of regular sleep cycle to stay alive.

These findings suggest that zombies may be able to slow their cellular breakdown by mimicking the survival techniques of the living. However, this doesn't necessarily mean a traditional, tucked-in-bed, eight-hour recharge for our undead friends.

Think of it as the standby mode on your computer. The machine hasn't shut down completely but is in a holding pattern, allowing it to last longer and run more efficiently when booted back up. Many insects and fish species act similarly, and so, too, may zombies. This would explain why they are often seen to be hardly moving at all when not in pursuit of prey.

Biologist Michael Harris suggests that zombies may be exhibiting a form of reduced metabolic state distinct from sleep, called mammalian torpor:

Torpor is a part of hibernation which, when exhibited by small mammals, leads to much reduced metabolism and reduced responsiveness. When exhibited by large

mammals the result is reduced metabolism and increased
longevity, but with maintained responsiveness.

So the next time you spot a zombie milling about aimlessly, don't just assume it's too stupid or slow to do anything else. Maybe it's just recharging so it can be refreshed and ready when the next tasty meal happens by.

RIGHTS OF THE INFECTED

 If a person infected with zombie pathogens shows no sign of illness for an extended period of time, then there are many important questions to address. What are the rights of the infected? What liberties should be granted to people who have contracted the zombie illness but are not yet dead or dying? Who gets Bill's stuff once we blow his head off?

If society does not collapse under the weight of a zombie pandemic, then the problem of what to do with thousands, or even millions, of friendly, everyday folk who just happen to have contracted a slow-acting, contagious disease that will eventually turn them into undead beasts may well become very real and very persistent. Do we shoot them on sight? Do we lock them up and throw away the key? What if they can live regular lives, with no sign of illness, for years? What if they can't even pass on the contagion until the very latest stage of their own progression?

In the closest model for this potential reality, John Tayman's bestselling work, *The Colony*, chronicles a dark chapter in Hawaiian history when thousands of lepers were forced to live on a remote island, separated from their families and doomed to eke out their remaining days in deplorable conditions. Their sickness was ruled an illegal act, their rights were stripped, and they were treated as living corpses:

> The patients were judged to be civilly dead, their spouses granted summary divorces, and their wills executed as if they were already in the grave.[24]

No matter how they were legally defined, the lepers were still alive when they were shipped away from the world. In fact, many lived years or decades in isolation, making them the first true example of the walking dead. It takes little imagination to see that the governmental and public response to the dreaded leprosy of old may be shockingly similar to that of the coming zombie pandemic.

But if she was bitten, and thus infected by an Unconsecrated, there are only two options. Kill her now or imprison her until she turns and then push her through the fence.
—The Forest of Hands and Teeth (2009), Carrie Ryan

The current malaria pandemic is a contemporary reminder of the challenges we will likely face when dealing with the rights of the infected. The World Health Organization estimates that there are as many as 500 million cases of malaria with more than 1 million resulting deaths each year. In fact, in Africa, a child dies from malaria every thirty seconds, and because the disease is transmitted by mosquito, it infects new victims without their knowing. Even though malaria patients are not themselves contagious, meaning that the disease cannot be transmitted directly from person to person, many face poor treatment upon diagnosis. They are locked away from society, stripped of their rights, and left to die in what amounts to sealed prison cells. This does nothing to stop the spread of the disease but is simply an irrational reaction to the public's fear and panic.

If a zombie pandemic hits with the same potency and spread as the current malaria crisis, there's no telling to what lengths people will go to protect themselves from infection. Sure, little Jimmy down the street may just be showing the first signs of illness, and sure, you may know full well that he doesn't even run the risk of developing full-blown zombieism for years to come, but don't be surprised if you find yourself screaming for his head with the rest of the mob as you bash in his parents' front door.

13: INFECTION SOURCES

Think an undead virus isn't possible? Researchers at the Herzberg Institute of Astrophysics in Canada claim that even though microbes are dead, they carry enough genetic information to allow new life to spring from their ashes. Team lead astronomer Paul Wesson even asserts that all life on earth may have originated from dead alien viruses that reanimated after reaching our planet:

> The vast majority of organisms reach a new home in the Milky Way in a technically dead state. Resurrection may, however, be possible.[25]

Wesson's hypothesis is highly speculative because we know so little about the true origins of life on earth. Nonetheless, if reanimated creatures are at the root of human civilization, it could be argued that the coming zombie plague is not only possible but likely. What's more, we may already have the sickness inside our very DNA.

In 2010, researchers from Osaka University in Japan accidentally discovered the gene sequence of the deadly borna virus buried inside the human genome. That means that every person on the planet is intimately connected to this virus in a way previously thought not possible.

Scientists have found upward of 100,000 elements of human

DNA that probably originated from viruses, but the borna virus belongs to a type that has never been found in the human genome before. Its discovery raises the possibility that many more viruses are still left unfound.

In some species, the borna virus is harmless, but it drives infected horses insane, causing them to commit suicide by smashing in their own skulls or starving themselves to death. It has also been linked to schizophrenia and bipolar disorder in humans.

Though the borna virus holds little promise of someday mutating into a zombie-causing agent, this new field of research brings up questions about where and how the undead threat will make itself known to an unprepared human race.

MUTATING PROTEINS

A prion is an infectious agent composed primarily of protein. It has been implicated in a number of deadly diseases in mammals, such as mad cow. All known prion diseases affect the structure of the brain, and all are untreatable and fatal.

Now a disturbing new strain of mad cow in humans, variant Creutzfeldt-Jakob disease (vCJD), has proven to infect and kill younger people, cause much more gruesome symptoms, and be transmitted from person to person in new and deadly ways.

The Centers for Disease Control and Prevention confirms that vCJD is an invariably fatal brain disease, with an incubation period measured in years, and an unconventional transmissible agent. The new dangers of this strain are echoed by the United States National Institutes of Health:

It may be possible to transmit vCJD through blood and related blood products such as plasma. Some animal studies suggest that contaminated blood may transmit the disease. Furthermore, scientists have no way of determining whether fluids are infectious or not.

The rapid evolution of the prion that causes vCJD has alarming implications for the study of zombieism. If vCJD becomes easily transmitted from one human to another through casual and/or sexual contact, like HIV, it could spell certain death to massive segments of the global population. Worse still would be an airborne prion disease driving people violently insane without the need for direct contact with the infected.

In January 2011, a study published in the journal *PLoS Pathogens* showed that not only can deadly prions be transmitted through blood, saliva, feces, and urine in mice but also through aerosols. This means that prion diseases have the potential to spread over vast distances like other airborne contagions.

In 2010, scientists at the Scripps Research Institute in Florida discovered that prions can develop large numbers of mutations. Through natural selection, these mutations can lead to evolutionary adaptations previously thought not possible. Charles Weissmanz, the head of the Scripps Department of Infectology and the study's lead author, says:

It was previously thought that once cellular prion protein was converted into the abnormal form, there was no further change. But there have been hints that something was happening. Now we know that the abnormal prions replicate, and create variants.[26]

Though prions are technically lifeless, possessing no DNA or RNA, it turns out that they are still somehow able to evolve.

As they mutate in new and unforeseen ways, the likelihood increases that a prion-based zombie sickness will someday show its ugly head.

If we consider a disease, possibly a prion disease, that shuts down most of the brain and most of the organs and retains just the minimum amount necessary to accomplish a primal need—that of feeding—then you can at least construct a theory.

—Zombie CSU *(2008)*, Jonathan Maberry

VIRUSES, BACTERIA, AND SPORES

 Researchers at the National Academy of Sciences have discovered a dangerous new trend in the evolution of the flu virus. By creating a hybrid virus that joined the deadly bird-flu strain with the more common human flu, they proved that not only is this union possible in nature, but it could also produce devastating results.

Bird and swine flu are extremely deadly, but in their current state, they don't spread easily from person to person. By contrast, human influenza is highly contagious but isn't usually potent enough to cause widespread death. When these two strains are combined, a new and virulent threat is born.

Asked about the possibility of different flu strains mixing, Hong Kong University virologist Yi Guan responded that if that happens, he will retire immediately and lock himself in a sealed laboratory, because it will likely mark the end of the world.[27] Strong words from a normally stoic scientist.

Applied to the study of zombies, the notion that several

different strains of the same root virus can merge has profound implications. If zombieism is simply a highly mutated variation of rabies, mad cow, or even influenza, then this dormant strain has only to mix with its more common cousin to create an instant pandemic the likes of which the world has never seen.

Samita Andreansky, a virologist at the University of Miami's Miller School of Medicine in Florida, claims that even pathogens that are not similarly rooted can be combined rather easily:

> *This is the age of microbiology. We can clone animals and humans in the lab, so we can certainly combine a highly virulent strain of rabies with a highly virulent strain of influenza.*[28]

Combining the symptoms of rabies with the infectiousness of the flu virus could initiate a zombie plague that is faster-acting and more lethal than ever thought possible.

Rather than needing a bite to become infected, a single sneeze could create dozens more zombies-to-be. Hundreds of thousands of seemingly healthy people would be unknowingly doomed by their inadvertent exposure. The implications for the human race of an airborne zombie virus are devastating.

....

ROMERO'S RULES

Romero's zombies are not a result of any contagious pathogen but, rather, a universal affliction that infects all living humans. In his first film, *Night of the Living Dead*, he suggests that a radioactive satellite crashing into the earth sparked the doomsday plague, but subsequent films don't address the root cause. To Romero, the only important fact is that everyone will someday become a zombie.

....

THE LAB GONE WRONG

Along these lines, researchers at Stanford University are making fundamental changes to the DNA of a deadly parasite, and their work has all the hallmarks of a classic zombie-outbreak story.

Toxoplasma gondii is a microscopic parasite that causes toxoplasmosis in humans and animals, which is the third leading cause of death from food-borne illness in the United States. Though often not fatal, according to the Centers for Disease Control and Prevention, the parasite remains inactive in the host body, waiting for the ideal time to reactivate itself. An estimated 60 million men, women, and children in the United States carry the parasite without even knowing it.

Toxoplasmosis drastically changes the behavior of rats and mice, making them drawn to the scent of cats, rather than fearful of it. Once the rodent is killed and eaten by a cat, the controlling parasite can then reproduce in its new host.

In humans, mild cases of infection can result in reckless behavior, including higher levels of aggression, jealousy, and paranoia. It can also cause inflammation of the brain, neurologic diseases, and other highly targeted disorders.

Could genetically altering a deadly, mind-controlling parasite be the first step toward the evolution of zombieism? If so, with a legion of people across the planet already infected, the newly modified organism needs only to link up with millions of ready victims.

TRIAL BY FIRE

It's generally believed that zombies can be safely dispatched with a little lighter fluid and a match. But what if the source of the undead plague can't be destroyed by fire? What if the sickness spreads even faster once ignited?

If we take as fact that zombieism is passed from one person to another through bodily fluids, then the sickness must exist on the microbial level. Microbes are single-cell organisms that live in the water you drink, the food you eat, and the air you breathe. Most microbes are helpful, but others have proven to be killers on a massive scale, including smallpox, flu, tuberculosis, malaria, plague, measles, and cholera.

Though most microbes can't survive fire, extremophiles actually thrive in extreme conditions that would kill other life forms. It's quite probable that the infectious agent in zombies is burned up right along with the body, but it seems possible that all or part of it could survive. An inhaled particle or an inadvertent rub of your eye, and you could be doomed to suffer a slow sickness, death, and reanimation without ever having come into direct contact with a zombie. So if you ever find yourself in a catastrophic zombie outbreak and a member of your group wants to torch the entire neighborhood, you might want to think twice about handing over the gas can. It could spell the beginning of the end for you, your loved ones, and everyone else for miles around.

Zombi 3 (1988)

DOCTOR: Our instruments have detected an enormous radioactive cloud in the air.

SOLDIER: That's not the worst of it. There've been numerous incidents of inexplicable murders reported throughout the area, and people are eating each other.

MORTON: We'll have to cut off the epidemic area.

DOCTOR: Cut it off, how?

ZOMBIE IMMUNITY AND CURE

If the zombie infection evolves from a known pathogen, could you be immune? Research done by the United States Air Force found that roughly 1 percent of the global population is incapable of contracting the HIV virus because of a genetic mutation. These mutated human cells have a slightly different structure from most, preventing the invading HIV cells from finding a suitable spot to attach themselves. Imagine plugging the wrong charger into your cell phone. No matter how hard you try, you're never going to get a good connection. The port and the attachment just don't fit.

The uncovered immunity to HIV and similar findings in leukemia and other cancers have had a profound influence on the way we look at disease and the future evolution of treatment strategies. Some experts go as far as to suggest that for every ailment, there is someone who is immune, and we just haven't tracked them all down yet.

Could it be that not only is a certain small percentage of the population immune to becoming zombies but those people may also hold the key to developing a working vaccine that could help prevent new zombie infections from spreading?

Following this logic, in 2010, researchers at Rutgers University figured out how RNA viruses are able to replicate, a discovery that could eventually lead to cures for the diseases they cause. Study director Nihal Altan-Bonnet explained that these viruses, including polio, SARS, and HIV/AIDS, copy themselves by taking a naturally occurring enzyme hostage:

> The goal of any virus is to replicate itself. For its replication machines to work, the virus needs to create an ideal lipid environment, which it does by hijacking a key enzyme from its host cell.[29]

By blocking a virus from gaining access to the necessary enzyme, these serious diseases would suddenly not be able to synthesize their viral RNA and replicate.

If the zombie plague is also viral in nature and if it uses the RNA platform, these findings could lead to the development of viable treatment options for the newly infected. Treated individuals could house the zombie sickness in their blood, could potentially be contagious, but would not ever get sick, die, or reanimate.

KNOW YOUR ZOMBIES: THE CLOWN

Zombieland (2009)

The plague in *Zombieland* is caused by a mutated form of mad cow disease that turns those infected into raving lunatics with an appetite for human flesh. Its great box-office success solidified the living zombie's place in the subgenre and proved once again that just because the world is dead doesn't mean you can't have a little fun.

Geeky hero Columbus reveals that the only thing he fears more than zombies is clowns. Unfortunately, to save the girl of his dreams he has to fight a snarling zombie clown on its home turf: an apocalyptic amusement park.

ILLUSTRATION BY LUCAS CULSHAW

14: THE END IS NIGH!

Unlike werewolves and vampires, zombies aren't interested in going to high school with you. Their cover isn't to become a star on your basketball team, an eccentric antiques dealer, or a singer in a rock band. Werewolves and vampires might be scary, but ultimately they're trying to coexist in a society in which they have a stake. By contrast, zombies don't know and don't care. Zombies don't have a cover. Instead, they have the singular mission of killing and eating every last living human on earth and will stop at nothing to accomplish their goal.

That's why when thinking about zombies, it's impossible not to think also about the end of the world. No other contemporary monster is so closely tied to complete societal collapse followed by the speedy extinction of the human race. It's a compelling scenario played out countless times on-screen and in print and is a fundamental principle of the modern zombie.

Zack Snyder, director of the highly successful remake of George Romero's *Dawn of the Dead* (2004), was drawn to zombies specifically because they embody our concerns about the rapid fall of modern civilization:

> *I have a feeling that our whole way of life is like an eggshell that we think is so impervious, but once you put a crack in it everything comes apart pretty quickly.*[30]

It seems Zack isn't alone in his thinking. On the heels of the tsunami and resulting nuclear disaster in Japan in March 2011, *Newsweek* magazine's cover simply read, "Apocalypse Now," asking what the #@%! could possibly be next. Author of *The End of the World as We Know It* Daniel Wójcik points out that fears about mankind's doom pervade modern popular culture in large part because they are backed by our experiences in an uncertain world:

> *The destruction of our environment, the greenhouse effect, the AIDS epidemic, widespread famine, overpopulation, incurable strains of pneumonia, Ebola and flesh-eating viruses, and other as yet unimaginable future afflictions may contribute to our eventual extinction.*[31]

In a grim forecast, Jared Diamond says that there is a strong possibility of the collapse of civilization within the next few decades. And far from being a survivalist nut-job or doomsday alarmist, Diamond is a Pulitzer Prize winner who was awarded the United States National Medal of Science by President Clinton in 1999. Do you plan on being around for the next thirty years or so?

Zombies vs Robots vs Amazons, Issue 3 (2008)

PIP: So it's really dead, isn't it?

BERTIE: What's dead? The bald zombie?

PIP: The world.

BERTIE: As it was, yeah.

If zombies are to cause the end of the world, some say they will rise when a current human virus horribly mutates. Others say a strange new type of infection in animals will jump species to deadly effect. Still others point to dangerous advances in biological warfare as a logical launch point. In truth, there's no telling what the final trigger of the next great undead outbreak will be.

Taking a cue from Diamond, I believe a certain level of paranoia can prove helpful in identifying the coming zombie pandemic in its earliest stages. I believe in turning over every stone and exploring every possibility, no matter how unlikely. When it comes to zombie research and survival, I'm not interested in wading through the rubble of mankind, scratching my head, and wondering what happened after the fact. The time for wild speculation and heated debate is now, because once the dead come knocking, all bets are off.

A DEADLY VIRUS ESCAPES!

Though the idea that government researchers will accidentally cause a zombie outbreak is arguably overplayed in the  movies, recent findings suggest that it might nonetheless be right on the nose. A 2010 article in *New Scientist* magazine provides evidence that a planned bio lab funded by the United States is almost guaranteed to result in disaster.

Foot-and-mouth disease is a highly contagious, often fatal viral threat that infects animals such as cattle, sheep, pigs, bison, and deer. It can be devastating to livestock and wild herds if left unchecked.

By the government's own risk estimates, the proposed research lab has a 70 percent chance of accidentally leaking foot-and-mouth, causing up to $50 billion in damage. But even that wasn't enough to kill the project. Now the National Academy of Science (NAS) says the risk is much higher, explains academy member Jack Roth:

If the virus that causes FMD escaped, it's likely it would reach distances far away before we knew it had escaped.[32]

NAS goes on to claim that the Homeland Security analysis is incomplete and utterly fails to learn from fifteen other past catastrophic accidents, almost ensuring future disaster.

Though foot-and-mouth has no clear connection to zombie-ism, the weight of the evidence makes it difficult to doubt that irresponsible research and incompetent safety strategies could eventually lead to the end of the world one way or another.

The Italian Zombie Movie (2009)

ROGERO: You know what that means. That means this is it. Armageddon. The apocalypse. The end of the world.

MARIA: Rogero, don't you think you're overreacting?

ROGERO: Overreacting? How can one possibly overreact to the end of the world!

In a scene frighteningly similar to *28 Days Later*, a group of fifteen monkeys at an isolated research lab in Japan's Aichi Prefecture escaped in July 2010 by catapulting themselves over a high electric security fence. The monkeys did so by bending and releasing flexible tree limbs. Though the monkeys were quickly rounded up, we can't help but imagine the consequences if they'd escaped to civilization carrying with them some new and deadly sickness or experimental bio-weapon.

In another case out of Japan, leading Asian news outlet the *Japan Times* filed a 2010 report about disturbing new symptoms observed in a high number of recently flu-infected people in that country:

The health ministry has reported that 151 flu patients up to age 17 demonstrated abnormal behavior between late

September and mid-November, including acting violently insane and uttering gibberish.[33]

Though authorities claim that the popular vaccine Tamiflu was at fault, leading to the ban of its use by teens, only twenty-six of the known "zombie flu" sufferers had ever used that specific drug. Something more complicated, and potentially dangerous, appears to be at work.

WE'RE ASKING FOR TROUBLE

Providing yet another sign that the human race is doing everything it can to speed up the arrival of the coming zombie plague, researchers in England recently discovered a new kind of superbug living inside the artificially enhanced breasts, butts, and noses of plastic-surgery patients. The deadly bug, which originated in south Asia, is resistant to nearly all antibiotics and is expected to spread across the entire planet before too long.

The offending agent is actually a gene known as NDM-1 and is unique because it can jump across different species of bacteria and is virtually untreatable. The new NDM-1 bacteria is resistant even to carbapenems, a group of antibiotics often reserved as a last resort for emergency treatment for multi-drug-resistant bugs.

Experts suggest that the proliferation of these superbugs could become a catastrophic global public-health crisis as the NDM-1 gene fuses with other deadly bacteria or even new pathogens that have yet to be identified.

If the undead sickness is caused by a bacterial agent that can be treated through modern medicine, the introduction of this newly discovered gene would turn a small and controllable outbreak into a global zombie pandemic that threatens the very survival of the human race. Hope those fake boobs were worth it!

Do you know how many thousands of people got illegal organ transplants in those early years leading up to the Great Panic? Even if ten percent of them were infected, even one percent.

—World War Z *(2006), Max Brooks*

From elective surgery to lifesaving organ transplants, the Centers for Disease Control and Prevention recently reported that a rare infection has been passed through organ donation, in what is the first human-to-human transfer of the deadly amoeba known as *Balamuthia mandrillaris* (BM).

BM causes a condition leading to focal paralysis, seizures, and other serious brain-stem symptoms, before eventually killing its victim. It also often creates skin lesions on the body and face, through which the amoeba may enter the blood-stream and migrate to the brain. Dr. Mark Jacobson notes that the process of infection is of primary concern:

Four people got organs from the deceased, and already two are showing signs of infection. Organs are not routinely tested for less common pathogens, which allows rare and deadly organisms to slip through.[34]

This raises the specter of lifesaving interventions becoming transmission points. Innocent people from across the country and around the world would accept infected organs, sealing their undead fate with what they believe to be a lifesaving surgical procedure.

Families staying home to help loved ones recover would run a serious risk of being attacked and eaten by their fathers, mothers, children, and siblings. Given the right incubation period, zombieism could take root in unsuspecting cities and towns before any warning signs were spotted or alarms signaled.

It approached the ancient woman slowly, moving only slightly faster than she. The figure had long, white hair and horrible skin. It was also very, very thin. I thought of those "after" pictures of meth addicts.
— Zombie, Ohio (2011), Scott Kenemore

For perhaps the most disturbing trend in recent years, we look to African drug addicts. In a grotesque display of ingenuity, desperate addicts are injecting themselves with other addicts' blood in an attempt to share the high. Called flashblood (or flushblood), the practice almost guarantees that users will contract AIDS and hepatitis from their infected donors, as reported by the *New York Times*.

A woman who has made enough money to buy a sachet of heroin will share blood to help a friend avoid withdrawal. The friend is often a fellow sex worker who has become too old or sick to find customers.[35]

There are even reports of addicts selling their blood on the black market.

Mixing blood types in large enough doses is deadly, but no one has ever tested the effects of mixing different types of blood, each carrying different deadly infections, and then cross-mixing that over an extended population. In short, flashblood is just another indication that the human race is doing a disturbingly good job of creating prime conditions for the dead to rise and eat us all.

15: ZOMBIELIKE CREATURES

A parasitic fungus in Thailand has scientists baffled, as it infects helpless carpenter ants and inexplicably turns them into the walking dead. Once infected, the ants are compelled to climb down from their natural canopy home, latching on to low leaves just before they die. Assistant professor of entomology and biology at Penn State University David P. Hughs has studied the phenomenon extensively:

> The fungus accurately manipulates the infected ants into dying where the parasite prefers to be, by making the ants travel a long way during the last hours of their lives.[36]

After the ant dies, the fungus is careful to preserve its outer shell, reinforcing weak spots to protect against invading microbes and other fungi. Growing inside the carcass for a week or two, fungal spores then fall to the forest floor to infect new ants.

The scientific study of zombies is largely an exploration of all that is strange and disturbing in our natural world and often leads to more questions than answers. There is no better example than the many zombielike creatures living on land and at sea across the globe.

CREATURES ON LAND

AMBER SNAILS

Tiny eggs from parasitic flatworms are ingested by the amber snail, later to hatch in its digestive tract. The larvae then change into sporocysts, causing drastic mutations in the snail's brain and physiology. Healthy snails seek darkness to hide from predators, but the infected amber snail moves itself into dangerous open space and light. It is also helpless to retract its newly swollen, pulsating tentacles.

The end result is that feeding birds mistake the exposed tentacles for a caterpillar or grub and rip them off the snail's defenseless head. The flatworm then grows to maturity inside the bird, laying eggs that are released in droppings for new snails to consume, and the disturbing cycle continues.

SCREW WORMS

Zombies are unique in that they are thought to eat only living human flesh, while most animals kill their prey before feasting. But the undead share a dietary interest with the common screw worm.

Screw worms are parasitic maggots that eat only the living flesh of warm-blooded animals. While other species of maggots feed on dead flesh, such as a rotting piece of meat or a putrefied wound, screw worms attack healthy tissue. The larvae hatch and burrow deep into the tissue as they feed, making them capable of causing severe tissue damage or even death.

If not quickly treated, a screw-worm attack will leave the host mortally wounded in a matter of days, and as the maggots become flies, dozens of additional victims will quickly be needed to support the growing population. The exponential model of a screw-worm outbreak is disturbingly similar to projections of a potential zombie sickness.

LAB RATS

It's widely believed that the driving force behind a functioning zombie is its brain, so whatever root sickness causes zombie-ism is likely controlling the body from there. With that in mind, a team of researchers at Stanford University created zombie rats by using a virus to insert genes into a specific part of a rat's brain, encoding a new reaction to certain colors of light.

Team leader Karl Deisseroth explained that shining the specific color of light onto a modified rat causes neurons in the primary motor cortex to fire.[37] The result is a rat that in-voluntarily runs around on command. Admittedly, this differs from common depictions of the modern zombie, because the undead are not normally controlled by an external force. But it's disturbing that a virus was used to deliver the controlling gene into the rat's neurons.

CREATURES AT SEA

LORICIFERA

Skeptics often point to the widely held belief that zombies don't breathe as proof of their impossibility. They note that in all of human history, no complex creature has been found that didn't rely on oxygen to function. But this argument was dealt a crushing blow in 2010, when researchers from Italy's Polytechnic University discovered the first-ever oxygen-free animal.

Though some types of bacteria and other single-celled organisms can live without oxygen, it was previously believed that nothing as complex as this newly discovered phylum,

Loricifera, could possibly exist on earth. Lead researcher Roberto Danovaro points out that the discovery of these life forms opens new perspectives for the study of all life.

While every other animal converts oxygen and nutrients into chemical energy for survival, Loriciferans get their considerable energy by internally creating molecular hydrogen. If the infectious agents behind zombieism function in a similar manner, then the undead body might be freed of its dependence on a constant flow of oxygen after reanimation.

ROTIFERS

If there have been scattered zombie outbreaks throughout history, it seems possible that an undead pathogen may have the ability to remain dormant for extended periods of time. In 2010, researchers at Cornell University found that at least one species of complex animal has the ability literally to turn into dust.

The aquatic bdelloid rotifer escapes mortal danger by transforming into dried particles and floating off into thin air. The rotifers remain in this passive state until they happen to fall into a habitable body of water that is free of any predators, then suddenly and mysteriously reanimate.

If the walking-dead sickness is able to mimic this newly discovered process, its disappearance and reappearance throughout history would be explained. Zombies that can't find food or are set on fire or even shot in the head could deteriorate to dust before the pathogen simply drifted away. Once external conditions were right, the sickness would then reappear to infect new victims and continue its morbid destruction.

HAIRWORMS

For yet another disturbing display of zombie-like behavior in the animal kingdom, we need look no farther than the parasitic hairworm. The worm develops to maturity inside an un-suspecting cricket on land but must live its adult life in water.

To make this transition, it takes control of the cricket's brain and forces it to commit suicide by leaping into an available pool or pond. Once in the water, the cricket quickly drowns, allowing the hairworm to emerge and swim away in search of a mate, having grown up to ten times as long as its host. Gross!

Ultimately, we won't know if the next great zombie plague will be delivered to mankind through insect, virus, bacteria, or rogue protein. Only by exploring all the possibilities and developing reasoned theories can we hope to have any chance of surviving when that final day comes.

SECTION III

ZOMBIE SURVIVAL

In Cormac McCarthy's Pulitzer Prize–winning novel turned film *The Road*, a father and son try to escape the bitter cold of a postapocalyptic winter by heading south on foot across what used to be the United States. They struggle on a daily basis to find food, water, and shelter while ducking violent, cannibalistic nomads who wander the countryside looking for fresh human flesh to eat. Sounds a lot like a zombie story, right?

McCarthy doesn't introduce a single zombie in his book yet still manages to paint a more realistic picture of an undead planet than much of the zombie literature produced in the past several years. In fact, with the slightest tweak to some minor characters and no change to the plot or core message, *The Road* would instantly become one of the best zombie novels ever written.

When I mentioned to my wife that one of the main characters in *The Road* kills herself rather than face life in such deprived times, she said she'd do the same thing in a heartbeat. Her exact words were:

When the dead rise, I'll still want my hot showers and happy hour. I'll definitely want to die if I don't get either for a month, maybe sooner if the weather is bad.

And it seems she's not alone in her plan to end it all when zombies come shambling through our neighborhood. A 1998 study published in the *New England Journal of Medicine* found that people kill themselves in greater numbers in the aftermath of a serious disaster, citing an almost 70 percent increase in the year following a major earthquake. In fact, results from a variety of studies overwhelmingly suggest that social breakdown caused by a catastrophic zombie outbreak will result in skyrocketing suicide rates.

If you're in my wife's camp, then you can skip this section altogether. But if you're willing to slug it out, you should read on, even if you don't believe in zombies, because the techniques needed to survive a zombie outbreak are the same needed to survive any number of catastrophic natural or man-made disasters.

The Road (2010)

MAN: We have to. We will survive this. We are not going to quit. I'm not going to quit.

WIFE: I don't want to just survive. Don't you get it? I don't want to . . .

MAN: Listen to yourself. You sound crazy.

16: WATER TO DRINK

Max Brooks stands onstage before a packed lecture hall. He is the bestselling author of *Zombie Survival Guide*, the first in what is now a long list of zombie survival manuals, most of which are, in my opinion, poor imitations of Brooks's original work. Hundreds of college students fill every seat and crowd along the back wall in giddy anticipation. Some are dressed up like zombies or zombie killers. Some flip through dog-eared copies of the guide, as if cramming for the most important test of their lives. Some compare survival strategies in heated, whispered debate. Finally, Brooks steps to the center podium, and the room falls quiet. "What is the first thing you'll want to have with you in a zombie outbreak?"

Eager students shout out possible answers. *A machete! A tank! A shotgun! My mommy!* They laugh. They shift in their seats, looking about as suggestions fly from all corners of the room. A jock in the back thinks it must be Molotov cocktails. A young professor with a ponytail twirls a pair of night-vision goggles around his index finger. The housewife zombie in the second row with a human-brain Jell-O mold just wants a friend who runs slower than she does, so she can get away when push comes to shove. Brooks shakes his head. They're all wrong. Dead wrong. Without a word, he simply holds up the water bottle in his hand. He takes a sip, then holds it up even higher so everyone can see. "Water, people. Water."

As the most recognized name in zombie survival, Brooks isn't a student of some exotic martial art. He doesn't engage in advanced weapons testing at a secret desert compound. He hasn't trained his family to neutralize an approaching threat instantly with their bare hands. No. Instead, Brooks composts his kitchen waste. He grows home crops in the backyard. He worries about the preservation and storing of extra food and water for drinking and cooking. He rightly focuses on the clear connection between crisis preparedness and response strategies for more common man-made and natural disasters and the measures needed to survive an infestation of the walking dead. He understands that the basics are what keep you alive in a zombie outbreak, and lacking those basics will kill you faster than any undead horde ever could.

DEADLY DEHYDRATION

Symptoms of dehydration can manifest in just a matter of hours, starting with a persistent and intensifying thirst and building to fatigue, chills, and headache.  Nausea soon sets in, as your muscles cramp and you experience tingling of the limbs. If you can't find adequate drinking water, your situation will quickly deteriorate, leading to vomiting, racing pulse, vision problems, confusion, seizures, and even unconsciousness, and finally death.

On July 30, 1945, the USS *Indianapolis* was torpedoed and sunk in the Philippine Sea. Of the 900 men who abandoned ship, only 316 were still alive when rescue planes spotted them four days later. Though the constant threat of shark attack is what brought the ordeal global attention, as re-counted by the fictional salty sea captain in the film *Jaws*, de-hydration killed far more people than the sharks:

> *First your mouth turns to cotton. Your saliva turns thick and bitter, until it disappears altogether. You become aware of your tongue as a fat, dry thing barricading your air passage. Your throat dries out until you can't talk, and you feel a massive lump in your windpipe, forcing you to swallow again and again, and every swallow is painful, but the lump won't go away. Without tears in your tear ducts your eyelids begin to crack, and you might weep blood.*[38]

The survivors of the *Indianapolis* remember the mass delusions suffered by their fellow sailors. Men thought the water was fresh just below the surface. Some thought they could see land and swam off to their deaths. Others were sure that the water fountains on the sunken ship would still work. Dozens of men dived down all at once, never to be seen again. Ocean survival is clearly a unique situation, but even if you can find fresh water to drink, water-borne illnesses might pose as deadly a threat as having no water at all.

January 12, 2011, was the one-year anniversary of the devastating earthquake in Haiti that killed an estimated 300,000 people and crippled the country's already weak infrastructure. Even the presidential palace was reduced to rubble. But one year later, nearly every news outlet in the United States reported that the biggest threat to the lives of those who survived was a lack of clean drinking water.

David Walton is deputy chief of the Haiti mission for Partners in Health, a nonprofit relief organization. Speaking about the proliferation of cholera, he says that hundreds of thousands of people contracted the disease within months of the initial disaster, and once the problem starts, it's almost impossible to control:

> If cholera was introduced into the United States tomorrow, it wouldn't take root because we have great sanitation, we have potable water. If you look at a place like Haiti that is one of the most water-insecure nations in the world and one of the nations that has some of the worst metrics in terms of sanitation, this is the perfect setup for cholera to both spread like wildfire and set up shop for years to come.[39]

Walton's assessment is based on a functioning sanitation and municipal water system continuing in North America. But if systems fail in an undead outbreak, as will likely be the case, we in the industrialized world will find ourselves at serious risk of dying of dehydration caused by diarrhea and vomiting associated with any number of water-borne diseases such as cholera and dysentery.

AVAILABLE SOURCES

If you haven't stocked up on water in advance of the zombie plague, then you'll be on a forced march to find a ready source almost immediately. Common strategies include filling up bathtubs while the taps are still flowing, collecting rainwater, and looking for available pools.

The average home water heater holds 50 to 75 gallons, or 6,400 to 9,600 ounces. In simple terms, an adult male should drink roughly 64 ounces of water per day. So once the heater water has been properly purified, it should provide enough drinking water for two people to be fully hydrated for at least fifty days.

Start by shutting off the water and gas to the building. This may be contrary to instinct, but the danger of contaminated fluids compromising your existing reserves outweighs any potential benefit. Next, locate the building's water heater. It's a large metal tank, usually in the basement, utility closet, or laundry room.

Even if you have a tankless water heater in your own home, chances are you will find yourself on the run and hiding out in new and unfamiliar shelters before too long. Water boilers can serve as lifesaving wells in the dry urban-desert landscape.

Shane Painter, author of *The Urban Survivalist Handbook*, recommends finding a plot of open grass in the early morning when other options fail:

> Now take a sheet and begin dragging it over the grass to collect the dew. As the sheet becomes damp you can wring it out into a bucket. Depending on how big an area you are dragging you could get up to a gallon of water per day.[40]

In testing, this technique produced wildly varying results depending on climate and location.

Adequate drinking water is essential to buy you needed time to fashion weapons, communicate with other survivors, and develop a solid plan for escape or further fortification. It also prevents you from dying in just a matter of days.

PURIFY YOUR SUPPLY

According to the World Health Organization, 3.5 million people die each year from water-borne illness across the globe. In a zombie outbreak, even the fresh-looking water coming from a working kitchen faucet may hold sewage backup and other deadly toxic substances. It does no good to locate a ready source of water, such as a plugged gutter, rain bucket, or toilet bowl, only to have unseen microbes incapacitate anyone brave enough to drink. Boiling water is a solid option but not always possible. So what's the answer? Drink bleach.

Mixed in the correct ratio, unscented bleach added to water can kill any unwanted contaminants and render the source safe for human consumption. In rough terms, half a tablespoon of bleach mixed into five gallons of clear water (or 2.5 gallons of cloudy water) should do the trick. Stir in and let sit for thirty minutes. If the water does not have a chlorine smell when finished, add more bleach.

So, next time your buddy says that all he needs is his double-barrel shotgun and enough ammo to blow every zombie's head off from here to Cleveland, tell him that you're going to invest in a bottle of bleach instead, and you'll pray for him after he's killed by diarrhea-related dehydration from drinking the tainted water in his badass camouflage commando canteen.

If you're inclined to prepare your water-purification kit ahead of time, there are dozens of different filters and puri-fiers that can be easily found and purchased through a simple Internet search. But for solutions on the fly, coffee filters are good for cleaning turbid or muddy water, or even spare cloth-ing such as socks. Most important is that you assume that all water is in need of purification before drinking and take any steps at your disposal to purify it.

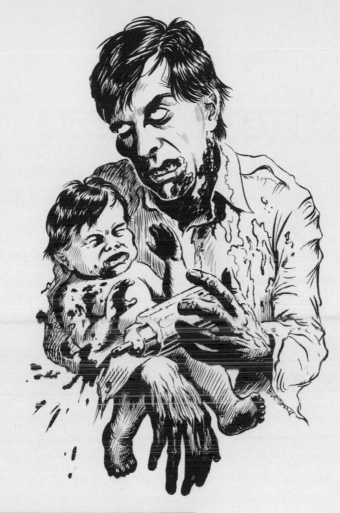

KNOW YOUR ZOMBIES: FLYBOY

Dawn of the Dead (1978)

As a helicopter pilot and one of the last remaining humans on earth, Flyboy is an unskilled survivalist who can't even shoot straight when his life depends on it. Played by David Emge, Flyboy goes from leading man to cult favorite zombie, lurching around in one of the most distinct zombie walks any actor has ever created.

Depicted here with a baby, Flyboy never gets to see his unborn child in the original film, but there is a zombie newborn in the *Dawn of the Dead* remake of 2004.

ILLUSTRATION BY THOMAS BROERSMA

17: PROTECTIVE SHELTER

In a zombie world, as in any extreme survival situation, the idea of shelter has to be thought of broadly. Shelter is any external protection from that which might do you harm. Forget about sleeping snug in your own bed or crashing on your neighbor's couch. Forget about pulling over to a roadside hotel after a long, hard day of travel. When the dead walk the earth, Motel 6 may quickly become a luxury beyond your wildest dreams.

Instead, think of shelter as an abandoned parking lot in the middle of a burned-out city. It's a fallen tree in the woods to shield you from harsh winds and rain. It's a pile of discarded roof shingles in the back corner of an old trash depot or the crawl space behind a sewer drain grate. Shelter is even the clothes on your own back or a found beach towel cut into strips and wrapped around your aching, swollen feet.

We lived on canned food and we listened to the radio in the dark, listened to static when that was all there was, hoping to hear of shelter somewhere, real shelter.
> —Dead Man's Land *(2009)*, David Wellington

SURVIVAL CLOTHING

I love zombie movies. I love the classics. I love the new stuff. I even love the crap that nobody else loves. And I understand that zombie movies are meant to entertain, not to provide sound survival advice, so it's unfair to judge them against real zombie-outbreak scenarios. Nonetheless, I'm always struck by the flawed actions that survivors in zombie movies continue to take long after learning the relevant facts about the threat they face, especially when it comes to clothing. Their critical errors in judgment and preparation inevitably cost more lives than the zombie menace would on its own.

This issue can be summed up in one simple question: If you were facing a deadly viral threat that could infect you with just a single drop of blood in your eye, don't you think you'd at least wear sunglasses?

In Danny Boyle's *28 Days Later*, a gang of survivors has plenty of time to spin whimsically around an empty, fully stocked grocery store, debating the merits of different types of liquor and chocolate, but somehow the concept of ducking into the sports shop across the street and grabbing a pair of ski goggles and maybe some racing leathers completely escapes them. What's more, the tough-as-nails lead female repeatedly hacks infected attackers to death wearing little more than a T-shirt, with nothing covering her face or mouth to protect against deadly blood spatter. This happens across all movies, from *Dawn of the Dead* (1978) to *Zombieland* (2009). The examples are endless. When the dead rise, if we as a society make as many silly mistakes about how to suit up as our cinematic counterparts, we'll all be toast.

Specific clothing needs are a function of location and climate, but there are basic rules of survival clothing that apply anywhere and in any disaster situation, and it all starts with your brain.

Human beings have big brains. That's our defining attribute. We are more intelligent than everybody else in the animal kingdom. Our bodies are designed to service that brain, providing the nutrients, oxygen, and protection it needs to function. Our bodies are not designed to keep us alive in extreme situations. We don't have a thick, furry hide to defend against the winter freeze like an Arctic fox's. We don't have the natural armor plating of a cockroach. We can't eject and regenerate body parts as the common lizard or a young spider does. Our smarts are supposed to keep us from freezing to death, being crushed, or losing limbs. So be smart.

Not only is an exposed forearm or calf easy pickings for that hungry zombie you just bumped into, but an untreated scratch or bug bite can lead to infection, debilitating sickness, and death. In an undead world, there's no hospital to visit if

you're feeling ill. There's no pharmacy stocked with antiseptic ointment. There's no friendly neighbor with a medical degree and a stocked first-aid kit. Tetanus shots, cough medicine, and penicillin will be long-forgotten remedies of a bygone age. Prevention is your last and only line of defense. Therefore, your skin should be thought of as a thin plastic bag holding your guts and bones in place. One accidental puncture, and your very life could leak out onto the floor like so much tomato soup.

Cover your head and feet at all times, thereby insulating you from the sun's harsh rays, preventing precious heat from escaping and acting as a primary first layer of combat protection. When possible, your entire body should be covered with loose, layered clothing in both hot and cold weather. Tight-fitting garments restrict blood flow and decrease your ability to regulate body temperature. Try to keep your clothes clean and dry. Dirt reduces the fabric's natural insulation qualities, and wearing wet clothing at night or in winter will turn you into a human Popsicle in no time flat.

If you have options, choose breathable fabrics like linen when exposed to extreme heat. In extreme cold, wool and synthetic material is the way to go. Cotton will suck your body heat if it gets wet, even from your own perspiration, and is commonly known as the "death fabric" in survivalist circles.

When it comes to zombie body armor, there is no need to strap on a full set of medieval chain mail or wear a full shark suit. A hooded sweatshirt with strips of industrial-strength tape could provide complete bite protection for your entire upper body. Add leather gloves and goggles, and you're well on your way to being virtually bite- and splatter-proof.

SURVIVAL HOUSING

Protective shelters also need to take into consideration your specific climate, but there is a basic set of criteria for sizing up the pros and cons of any undead shelter. The DSM Scale is a system that looks closely at three primary areas when evaluating the quality of a shelter. In order of increasing importance, they are:

1. *Defensibility.* What are the location's natural defensive advantages? What weapons can be found or created therein? What steps can be taken to eliminate vulnerabilities?
2. *Sustainability.* How much food and water is safely available? What essential supplies are stocked and ready? What threat does the surrounding environment pose both now and in time?
3. *Mobility.* Are there a number of adequate escape routes for safe retreat? What transportation options does the location

provide? Are the essential weapons and supplies able to be made portable?

While a discount retailer such as Costco may score high in defensibility, with available weapons and almost no vulnerabilities, its sustainability rating takes a hit because of the extreme threat presented by the surrounding area. In a zombie outbreak, big-box stores will draw a desperate and violent crowd, quickly becoming epicenters of death.

By contrast, a suburban home may have large windows and be difficult to defend, but if upgrades can be easily made, a supply of canned food and a backyard pool could allow for a period of relative safety. Of course, when it inevitably comes time to move, the water in the pool can't be carried along without portable containers and advanced planning.

DEFENSIBILITY

A good rule of thumb when planning your zombie shelter's defense is to hope for the best but prepare for the worst. Sure, the undead may be mindless drones that can't even complete the simple task of turning a doorknob, but what if they're not? What if zombies are smarter, faster, and more able-bodied than anyone ever imagined? How well will your defenses hold up if they're designed around the expectation of a lesser threat? I'd hate to be the one to find out.

Instead, think about what steps you would take if an angry mob of humans were coming to attack your shelter and kill you and your loved ones. In a land gone crazy, the likelihood that you will face both living and undead enemies is very real, so any survival strategy that doesn't account for the greatest possible threat is utterly useless.

Don't make the mistake of narrowly focusing on combat with zombies. Step outside yourself to imagine the complete pandemonium that will consume any infected area. Chaos will rule the day, and questions like these should be asked early and often: Can I break down this barricade? Can I climb over this obstacle? Can I breach this structure? Can my defenses be stronger?

In the end, the challenges ahead can't be fully understood until they present themselves. No one knows what's just around the corner in a time of law and reason, let alone when zombies are eating the neighbors across the street. When building defenses, all we can do is hope for the best and plan for the worst. But whatever you do, never underestimate how bad the worst can be in an undead world.

SUSTAINABILITY

In a zombie world, the power grid will inevitably fail, making night an extremely dark environment. Candles, flashlights, lamps, and other interior light sources will suddenly be the equivalent of a "Come loot me" sign to anyone searching for places to raid. Survival expert James Wesley Rawles says that your house should look anonymously dark, like those of your neighbors who have already run for the hills or are without power.

To avoid unwelcome guests, cover all windows with heavy black plastic sheeting. Trash bags, blankets, and other improvised blackout precautions tend to leak light, so if you don't have the proper material, you should consider illuminating interior windowless rooms only, and even that at a minimum.

Rawles goes so far as to recommend installing infrared, motion-sensitive floodlights to the outside of your house. Invisible to the naked eye, these lights will provide an early-warning system when used with night-vision goggles.

If you're like me and don't have high-tech gear at the ready, a less extreme alternative is to set up dummy lights in abandoned houses up the street or on another block. With good sight lines, you'll be able to monitor neighborhood activity from the safety of your blackened shelter.

But it wasn't a prank. And it didn't go away. Just a couple of days after the first internet videos appeared it was the lead story on the nightly news. And then everything just started shutting down.

—Zombie, Ohio *(2011), Scott Kenemore*

If the Internet is still working when things really go south, you might also want to consider disabling your Wi-Fi.

Wi-Fi signals can be used as primitive homing devices, making you vulnerable to attack from other hostile humans even if your house appears to be abandoned from the outside. All a clever looting gang needs to do is drive down residential streets with their laptop set to search for available Wi-Fi. A signal means jackpot for them and trouble for you.

Even if your house is completely blacked out, an active wireless network lets the bad guys know there's a potentially lucrative target in the immediate area. Once the gang gets a hint that someone is sheltering nearby, they'll search two or three likely houses until you're discovered. At that point, zombies are the least of your worries, as your food, water, and other supplies become a thing of the past.

So when the undead rise, consider plugging in or shutting down. Though the Internet may last longer than grid utilities such as power and water, it's not worth the risk as people become more and more desperate to survive. Besides, nobody will be reading your Facebook updates anymore, anyway.

MOBILITY

In an extreme survival situation, your shelter is only as good as its escape routes. No matter how secure it appears to be, if you can't get out in seconds, that perfect hideout could quickly turn into the perfect tomb.

Once your defenses are fatally breached, either by the undead or by other hostile humans, a "fire" plan should be put into action. Don't grab valuables or try to fight off the threat. Any movement not directly related to escape is a waste of time and energy. Every second counts! In less than thirty seconds, things can go from bad to worse to completely out of control.

When the dead walk, most of us won't have the advantage of living in a specially created zombie-proof structure. But even in the average home, there are concrete steps that you can take at the first sign of a zombie outbreak to ensure safe retreat should the need arise.

Closets are excellent pass-throughs to secured rooms or other levels entirely. In a two-story home with a basement, closets can be a safe connection between the second floor and the basement, bypassing the dangers of the ground floor altogether. For a single-story house without a basement, look for an internal closet to access the roof and any crawl space below the subfloor. You can then develop your escape strategy using these access points.

Build your "domestic tunnels" with a specific purpose in mind. A pass-through from the basement to the roof should be sealed at all other levels, with closet doors blocked up for safety. If access is required to the first floor, create another point in a different closet by punching out the ceiling there.

Other escape methods include portable ladders to climb down from second-story windows and roofs or steel and wood planks to bridge gaps between one structure and another. Whatever your strategy, the ability to flee any given location through multiple exits is essential. Do not bet your life and property on the hope that you won't be discovered or that your defenses will hold up to attack.

On the DSM Scale, I rank mobility well above the other two criteria in importance, because in a zombie catastrophe, no place is truly safe or secret.

BAD IDEA: ZOMBIE TIMESHARES

Business is booming for companies that build doomsday safe houses, but because of the high cost of construction, the new model is to buy part ownership in a larger facility designed to house up to two thousand people. The Vivos Network, for example, is a planned group of twenty fortified, underground living communities spread across the United States, intended to protect those inside for up to a year from any number of catastrophes.

But one overlooked issue is the massive amount of trust in strangers that these partial-ownership facilities require. When hundreds of people have the ability to access your shelter, what's to stop an owner from bringing his entire extended family along even though he's only purchased one spot? What's to stop dozens of owners doing likewise, thereby instantly shrinking your food supply from a year to just a couple of weeks?

By contrast, what if you have loved ones visiting when the dead rise? Will you bring them along or elect to follow the rules and leave Aunt Bertha outside to be eaten by zombies just because she doesn't have a golden ticket?

Add in the standard problems of clashing personalities, religious and political disagreements, and the inevitability of hidden infections in the group, and the community-shelter system seems like a disaster waiting to happen.

18: FOOD TO EAT

Lewis Keseberg was out of options. It was the winter of 1847, and he was trapped inside an isolated mountain cabin with a badly injured leg that rendered him unable to walk. Lewis and his young family were part of a group of eighty-seven pioneers bound for a new life in California when a storm trapped their wagon train in the snowy Sierra Nevadas. Those healthy enough to continue the trek were sent ahead for help, including his wife and children. Before she left, Lewis made a promise to his only daughter that he would survive at any cost.

The cabin was warm enough, and the falling snow provided plenty of water for drinking. But as the weeks turned into months, with still no sign of rescue, starvation and resulting sickness took hold of Lewis and the others left behind. The small band of survivors was reduced to just Lewis, lying on the floor surrounded by five corpses blankly staring at him, their gray skin stretched tight across exposed teeth and jutting bone.

By night, he would listen to wolves clawing at the door and roof in hopes of gaining access to a fresh meal. By day, he would boil and eat the flesh of his dead companions to stay alive. When Tamzene Donner returned from a nearby cabin, she refused to eat human meat and soon died herself, orphaning her five children. Lewis promptly ate her as well.

Keseberg was eventually rescued and rejoined his family

to lead a long and prosperous life in California. He was never convicted of any crime. And there is no question that if he had not engaged in cannibalism, he would have died along with so many others.

Coming back he found the bones and the skin piled together with rocks over them. A pool of guts. He pushed at the bones with the toe of his shoe. They looked to have been boiled.

—The Road *(2006), Cormac McCarthy*

If the next great zombie outbreak leads to societal collapse, food will instantly become a dwindling resource. In a matter of days, people across the planet will be forced to make new and difficult choices about what and whom to eat.

DEATH BY STARVATION

Human starvation is a three-tiered process. Initially, blood glucose levels are maintained by the liver, but because there is only enough stored glycogen to last a few hours, the second stage of starvation is quickly reached. Put another way, the feeling of hunger you get after time passes from your last meal is your body telling you it's reached the second phase of starvation and will literally begin to eat itself if not given more food. This is when a person's fat percentage comes into play.

The body begins to convert its fat reserves into fatty acids and glycerol to support muscle and brain function. Once the fat runs out, the third stage of starvation begins, and there is a switch to proteins as the major energy source. Muscles, the largest source of protein in the body, are rapidly depleted.

Needless to say, once your muscles are being eaten from

within, you're in big trouble. In fact, starvation-related death is often caused by heart failure, because the heart—a muscle—is broken down to the point of collapse.

Therefore, individuals with higher levels of body fat can last longer without food, because they remain in the second stage of starvation for more time than their skinny counterparts. What's more, those who fit into the obese category have a substantially increased life expectancy because of their ability to supply energy to the body by using up ample stores of fat.

Of course, if you're being chased by zombies, it doesn't hurt to be able to run fast and for long distances. But if you're locked in a safe place and forced to stay put even after food supplies have been depleted, you're better off packing a few extra pounds.

AVAILABLE OPTIONS

So what will you eat when the food runs out? The arrival of zombies will most likely give rise to a host of new staple proteins in the human food supply.

Columbia University estimates that there were 175 million rats in the United States in 2002, most of which lived in cities. That number continues to rise rapidly. In 2004, *National Geographic* estimated that there were more than 75 million feral cats nationwide. Today, for every human born in the United States, there are 45 cats born. An estimated 4.1 million human births each year equates to more than 184 million new cats.

In World War II, the Nazi siege of Leningrad resulted in food supplies being almost completely cut off from the city. Rations were quickly lowered to just a third of the daily amount needed by an adult. The city's population of dogs, cats, horses, rats, and crows disappeared within months as they became the main course on many dinner tables. Reports of cannibalism began to appear. Thousands died of starvation, upward of 75,000 in just sixty days. The frozen earth meant that their bodies could not be buried, so corpses accumulated in the city's streets, parks, and other open areas.

When civilization breaks down, the convenience of the corner burger joint and the well-stocked supermarket will quickly become a thing of the past. Will rat sandwiches and kitty pot pie be the new quintessential American foods? Or when the dead rise, will the only long-term alternative be to eat one another?

Zombieland (2009)

CLEVELAND:	What are we doing here?
TALLAHASSEE:	We're taking a look. That's a goddamn Hostess truck.
CLEVELAND:	Yeah, I see that. A Hostess truck, so what?
TALLAHASSEE:	I could use a Twinkie.

If you're planning ahead, one option to stave off hunger in the early days of the outbreak is a prepackaged meal plan. They offer an assortment of sealed, ready-to-eat food items that never spoil and can be stored virtually anywhere. A month's supply, which includes breakfast, lunch, dinner, and a snack, comes in a single smallish box that will fit in any closet. What's more, it's surprisingly light and can be carried by virtually anyone, male or female, large or small.

For disaster survival, consider ordering a single month, then canceling your account with no penalty. Buy it, store it, and forget about it. When the dead rise, you'll have at least two months of rationed food to keep you going while you worry about more pressing concerns.

Additionally, Emergency Ration Bars (ER Bars) are a useful meal substitute. Similar to those approved for use by the U.S. Coast Guard, they offer a disaster victim the right blend of required calories and nutrients to survive for three days. Packaged to store safely for five years, even in extreme temperatures and conditions, the ER Bar comes in either 2,400- or 3,600-calorie bricks. They even make bars specially formulated for your dog or cat.

With no tropical oils, nuts, or cholesterol, allergic reactions are not a concern, and unlike most other premade survival meals, the ER Bar doesn't require any water, heating, or other preparative measures before eating. Furthermore, each is enriched with 100 percent of your recommended daily vitamins and minerals.

LOOTING

Whatever your situation, don't count on looting needed food from the local mega-mart. An extensive analysis of injuries occurring in large crowds over the last three years found that from Boston to Beijing, people of all ages and walks of life actively participated in the deaths of their fellow man to accomplish their own often trivial objectives.

Innocent bystanders were trampled to death in Angola in March 2009 so that a mob could get a better view of the visiting pope. One month later, in the Ivory Coast, twenty-two people were killed in a stampede of soccer fans upset about their team's loss. In 2006, 346 pilgrims were crushed to death on the last day of their trip to Mecca. The list goes on and on.

But perhaps the most telling example is that of Jdimytai Damour, a 270-pound Walmart worker who died on November 28, 2008, after being trampled by suburban Long Island shoppers looking to take advantage of early holiday discounts. Even the paramedics who unsuccessfully attempted to revive Damour were jostled by the aggressive crowd.

If everyday citizens are killing one another just to get a better price on a flat-screen television, imagine what ugly behaviors will surface when actual survival is at stake. The findings suggest that "inadvertent human violence" may well be a greater cause of death and destruction than any flesh-eating zombie or lunatic with a shotgun in the coming undead pandemic.

THE IMPORTANCE OF FIRE

Personally, I've been slow to appreciate the full importance of fire in zombie survival. I live in a warm climate so I don't need fire for heat, I don't like hot drinks, and I even prefer my food cold. I'm the guy eating leftover pizza straight from the fridge or soup out of the can without heating it up.

I also strongly feel that attracting attention is the last thing you want to do in an undead world, and so the need for any fire must be weighed against the risks of detection by zombies or other hostile humans. But there's no question that mankind's ability to control fire separates us from the rest of the animal kingdom and is at the root of our impressive evolutionary and technological advance.

Richard Wrangham is a professor of biological anthropology

at Harvard University and author of *Catching Fire: How Cooking Made Us Human.* He argues that humans are so intimately tied to our diet of cooked food that it affects every aspect of our lives, both mentally and physically. Like cows eating grass or fleas sucking blood, we have adapted to eating cooked foods as our signature diet. It is woven into the fabric of what makes us human:

> *It is easy to forget what life would have been like without fire. The nights would be cold, dark, and dangerous, forcing us to wait helplessly for the sun. All our food would be raw. No wonder we find comfort by a hearth.*[41]

From cooking to warmth to water purification, anyone serious about surviving future natural disasters, social unrest, or a full-scale zombie pandemic should own a reliable fire kit. Like every other modern convenience in a zombie pandemic, gas burners, matches, and butane lighters will likely be a dwindling resource. For long-term fire needs, consider an artificial flint stick and metal striker that can be purchased for just a few dollars and will create great sparks on command. Or choose any of the dozen of other reliable survival fire-starting products available through a quick web search.

19: THE HUMAN THREAT

There's a lot we still don't know about zombies and cannot know until the dead rise. However, when taking a hard look at the specific makeup of the modern zombie, one key ingredient is as obvious as the nose on your face: people.

People make zombies. No matter what else is in the mix, without people, there can be no walking dead trying to hunt and kill other people. This seems like a simple concept, but it's too often overlooked when developing survival strategies for a zombie outbreak. The best advice for increasing your odds of staying alive, and the first thing to consider when developing a survival plan, is to keep away from people. Without people, there can be no zombies.

Therefore, banding together in large groups may be a bad idea. Finding refuge in any densely populated area such as a government camp, a city building, or a military base is inviting death. In fact, the classic cinematic image of a horde of zombies attacking a few people in an abandoned farmhouse presents exactly the wrong impression.

An abandoned farmhouse has two major advantages built right into its name: (1) it's abandoned, meaning no people, and (2) it's a farmhouse, meaning it is probably on a large plot of open land that provides good visibility and further decreases the likelihood of any other people being around. Not to mention the potential for growing food and access to an independent water supply. Unfortunately, abandoned farmhouses don't grow on trees. Necessity and geography will cause all of us to come into contact with other people sooner or later.

DESPERATE MEASURES

My neighbor Jim is a really nice guy. He, his wife, and their young son are all as friendly as can be. Jim knows that I hide my house key under the rock behind the overgrown spruce

bush and not in the plastic key holder shaped like a frog that sits by the front door. He even knows that I keep an empty key holder in plain sight in hopes that an assailant will check there, assume that the extra key has been removed, and give up searching. Better to point them in the direction you want them to look, rather than just let them look anywhere. I consider Jim a trusted friend.

But if a widespread zombie outbreak was quickly followed by a complete breakdown of our modern way of life, what would happen then? Would communities band together, providing support for one another in their time of need? Would neighbor help neighbor when food is running low and undead cannibals are roaming the streets? Would the spirit of cooperation rule the day? Would Jim resist the urge to take my last reserves of water for the good of his own family? The answer is a resounding no.

In speaking with dozens of disaster-response experts across the globe, I got the same basic response over and over again. Mass panic would lead to civil unrest on a global scale. Those few who had enough food and water would barricade themselves in their homes, only to be attacked by hostile humans desperate to save their own skin. Death would come knocking long before zombies ever did.

James Rush, team leader for the National Bioterrorism Hospital Preparedness Program, echoed these grim predictions:

> Cities would be extremely dangerous places, with widespread looting and violence. And the corresponding hospital systems that service those areas would be instantly overloaded and unable to cope.

Speaking on condition of anonymity, a senior official in the U.S. Department of Homeland Security confirmed his belief that rampant mob mentality would quickly lead to the breakdown of law and order. National Guard troops would be sent into urban areas to quiet the population, but their efforts would only lead to more bloodshed. Front-line personnel, such as police and medical first responders, would risk constant ambush for their vehicles, weapons, and supplies. In short, it would be a complete and total nightmare.

In line with expert predictions, 1978's *Dawn of the Dead* depicts a small band of survivors who find refuge from the zombie plague in a sealed shopping mall, only to be overrun by hostile human marauders who exploit the lawless environment to take what they want violently. *Dawn* is Romero's second zombie movie, considered by many to be among the best ever made.

So, if you think that being eaten alive will be your biggest problem when the undead rise, you might want to think again. What's more likely is that your house will be set on fire with you and your family inside, just because some desperate survivors think you might have something they want.

In fact, humans are arguably much more dangerous in a zombie plague than the undead horde itself. Zombies don't possess a human's ability to think, plan, plot, scheme, double-cross, negotiate, and cheat. Furthermore, zombies don't know where you hide your essential supplies and wouldn't be interested in stealing them even if they did.

ROMERO'S RULES

Romero is clear in all of his films that the zombies aren't the real threat and never really were. To him, the root cause of mankind's demise at the hands of the undead is our own selfish agendas and unchecked ego. Ultimately, we are the tools of our destruction, because we're not able to work together to eradicate the lesser evil: the zombies.

The seriousness of the human threat in a zombie outbreak cannot be overstated. We may not know exactly where the undead sickness will start or how it will spread, but one thing is certain: your fellow citizens will be the most dangerous thing you face in the early days of societal collapse.

It seems that every few weeks, we're given another reminder of this, and numerous reports out of the 2010 earthquake zone in Chile were no exception. On February, 28, 2010, *NBC Nightly News* had this to say about the situation there:

> *The real peril now is that the looting and violence is not confined to empty businesses but is also widespread in the homes of those who have survived. Basically a nightmarish scenario of neighbor against neighbor is unfolding.*[42]

Because of the breakdown in the distribution chain in Chile, people were desperate to secure food, water, and supplies for themselves and their loved ones. Even though they knew that the world wasn't coming to an end, that everything would eventually get back to normal, the drive for survival was too great for them not to take matters into their own hands.

In a zombie pandemic, we will have the same lack of supplies and services, with the added shock and fear that walking corpses bring. The peril faced by survivors of a zombie infestation at the hands of their neighbors will be exponentially greater than that of any more common disaster.

WHO IS TO BLAME?

When the dead rise, will it be your fault? Carey Morewedge of Carnegie Mellon University says that when things go bad, there is a human need to find someone to blame, and that spells further disaster in a zombie outbreak. His paper "Negativity Bias in Attribution of External Agency," published in the *Journal of Experimental Psychology*, explains that blame is our natural default setting because unexpected events are difficult to predict, and the unpredictable can be scary. What is more scary and unpredictable than an infestation of the walking dead?

> *No one knew what caused the outbreak. Some said it was radiation. Some said it was a crashed meteor affecting the earth. Some said it was the wrath of God.*
> —Graveyard Slot *(2005), Cavan Scott*

The Black Plague of the Middle Ages was the deadliest event in human history, with some estimates suggesting that

half of the world's population was killed off. Looking at societal reactions to such a devastating time, specifically the
blame trigger, can give insight into the challenges we may
face in the coming zombie pandemic.

As the very real notion of the end of the world set in at
the height of the Black Plague, many previously peaceful
people were sent into a religious panic that bordered on
sheer insanity. And no group better illustrates this point than
the flagellants.

The flagellants walked across Europe whipping themselves to a bloody pulp as they shambled through the streets
of any plague-infested town they passed. Their aim was to
atone for the sins of man that brought such suffering to them
all. But when masochism didn't work, they started to attack
and kill anyone they thought might be a particularly offensive
sinner. Even town priests were not safe from their wrath. As
the violent fervor intensified, the flagellant mob murdered
tens of thousands of innocent people before the plague began
to subside and the Catholic church ruled them heretics and
outlawed the practice.

But we don't need to look back hundreds of years in the
past to find irrational blame based on misguided religious
beliefs. On the January 13, 2010, episode of *The 700 Club*,
Pat Robertson openly blamed the Haitian people for the
devastating earthquake they had just suffered. Hundreds of
thousands of people were killed, and according to Robertson,
it was their own fault because they'd made a pact with the
devil years before:

> And you know, Kristi, something happened a long time ago
> in Haiti, and people might not want to talk about it. They
> were under the heel of the French, you know, Napoleon the
> Third and whatever, and they got together and swore a pact

to the devil. They said, "We will serve you if you'll get us free
from the French." True story. And so the devil said, "OK, it's
a deal."[43]

On that same program, just two days after the World Trade
Center attacks in 2001, Jerry Falwell blamed the tragedy not
on the foreign hijackers or distant terrorist masterminds but
on what he perceived to be the real homegrown menace:
homosexuals and feminists.

Irrational blaming in times of crisis crosses all cultures
and religions. A prominent Indian journalist, Rajeev Sriniva-
san, suggested that a 2004 earthquake and resulting tsunami
that killed more than 230,000 people in fourteen countries
was a sign of retribution against Christians in India, whose
activities he sees as betraying that nation's essentially Hindu
character. He referred to the event as the "Christmas quake"
and implied that the December 27 date was no coincidence.

A 2010 study from York University in England found that
sustained levels of anxiety can give rise to radical, violent
religious beliefs. Published in the *Journal of Personality and
Social Psychology*, the evidence suggests that anxious people
more fervently cling to their ideals and are more extreme
in their convictions. Lead researcher Ian McGregor explains
that a process known as Reactive Approach Motivation (RAM)
is to blame:

Reactive Approach Motivation is a tenacious state in which
people become "locked and loaded" on whatever goal or
ideal they are promoting. They feel powerful, and thoughts
and feelings related to other issues recede.[44]

McGregor adds that extreme stress in the face of danger
causes many to become both paranoid and more willing to

submit to the control of a charismatic external force, allowing cult leaders and doomsday prophets to flourish when the zombies come.

If you're not planning to join a cult with the rest of the crazies, you might want to think about keeping a low profile when CNN starts talking about dead people rising and attacking their neighbors. If not, you could find a bloodthirsty horde of freaks kicking down your door and burning you alive on the off chance that you caused the undead apocalypse.

KNOW YOUR ZOMBIES: KAREN COOPER

Night of the Living Dead (1968)

Karen Cooper is the first film character ever to turn into a modern zombie. Her parents frantically attend to a bite she's suffered, only to be killed and eaten by their little girl in the basement of a secluded Pennsylvania farmhouse. Still, Romero makes it clear in all of his zombie films that the human threat is much more deadly than any undead menace.

Though she never appears outdoors on-screen, a promotional photo of Kyra Schon as Karen standing in the farmhouse yard is one of the most iconic images from *Night of the Living Dead*.

ILLUSTRATION BY MATT GROLLER

20: SYSTEMIC COLLAPSE

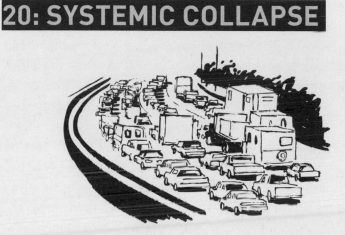

If you think you're going to be saved by the solid advice of your elected officials in a zombie outbreak, think again.

In late September 2005, Hurricane Rita was approaching Houston, Texas. With memories of Katrina's devastating impact on the Gulf Coast still fresh in the minds of public officials, dire warnings went out across the airwaves that implied that citizens needed to get out of town or die. Upwards of 2.5 million people jammed the roads, creating a colossal hundred-mile-long traffic jam that left many people stranded and out of gas for days.

Houston mayor Bill White, who originally called for the mass evacuation, soon admitted that the highway was a death trap. He said that his plan had not anticipated the volume of traffic, even though a simple math equation that measured the number of residents against the road capacity could have been successfully completed by the average middle school student.

In neighboring Baton Rouge, Louisiana, Governor Kathleen Blanco advised residents to "write their Social Security numbers on their arms in indelible ink" so that the medical examiner could identify their dead bodies after they were found drowned by floodwaters in their homes or bludgeoned to death by debris sailing on deadly winds. But then she and other officials seemed completely unprepared for the mass panic that ensued.

Back on the gridlocked highways of Texas, twenty-four elderly evacuees were killed when a mechanical problem ignited a fire on their charter bus. Rescue workers had no chance of reaching them through endless stalled traffic. They heeded the bad advice of their government representatives and paid the ultimate price. Be careful not to do the same.

No one knew what the next day would bring, how far the calamity would spread, or who would be its next victim, and yet, no matter whom I spoke to or how terrified they sounded, each conversation would inevitably end with, "But I'm sure the authorities will tell us what to do."
—World War Z (2006), Max Brooks

AN UNREADY GOVERNMENT

James F. Miskel served as professor of national security affairs at the U.S. Naval War College for twelve years and was also a member of the National Security Council under former presidents Ronald Reagan and George H. W. Bush. In short, he knows what he's talking about when it comes to issues of government preparedness in the face of a crisis. And that's what makes his insights on the topic so much more disturbing.

In his 2006 book, *Disaster Response and Homeland Security*, Miskel observes that government typically deals with past failures by adopting a narrow focus on specific problems and generating targeted solutions. But because no two catastrophes are ever the same, a new and unforeseen failure is always waiting just around the corner. In fact, this "fine-tuning" approach, coupled with a highly interdependent agency structure, practically guarantees that we won't be ready for the next surprise:

> *Benjamin Franklin defined insanity as expecting a different result after doing to same thing over and over again. This definition describes our approach to reforming the disaster relief program in the United States.*[45]

If the government isn't prepared to deal with the next big hurricane, earthquake, or terrorist attack, then how can we expect anything but confusion, communication gaps, and systemic breakdown when facing something as horrific as a zombie outbreak? Claims of a streamlined, vigilant post-9/11 government fall flat when compared to Miskel's mountain of hard evidence and reasoned insights.

---

28 Days Later (2002)

JIM: What about the government? What are they doing?

SELENA: There's no government.

JIM: Of course there's a government, there's always a government. They're in a bunker, or a plane.

MARK: No, there's no government. No police. No army. No TV. No radio. No electricity.

Not only is the government not prepared, but our own supply chain is at certain risk of total collapse.

Today all nations and most businesses operate on a management principle known as just-in-time. The guiding rule is to deliver goods and services on an as-needed basis. This process makes great financial sense because it eliminates expensive storage costs and future waste of unused product. However, just-in-time's overdependence on constant, reliable transportation creates an unsustainable need for massive quantities of oil. If the oil supply is cut off for any reason, the system is vulnerable to sudden and total collapse.

Now consider the workers it takes to make just-in-time function: truck drivers, packers, security personnel, forklift operators, dispatchers, maintenance crews, mechanics, and warehouse staff, just to name a very few. There are literally hundreds of people playing a direct part in getting a single banana, can of soup, or lightbulb to your door.

Current government estimates predict that essential services could be maintained only for a limited time if absentee rates rise above 25 percent. That's still three in every four people showing up on the job as normal after being informed that the dead have risen from the grave and are feeding on the living. Would you go to work under those conditions? Would anyone?

When the just-in-time supply chain falls, the end of our way of life will follow soon after. Well before the first zombie comes knocking, most people will have run out of food, fuel, power, and water. And when that happens, all the guns and ammunition in the world won't keep remaining perishable goods from spoiling, lights from going out, or desperate survivors from breaking down under the weight of malnutrition, dehydration, and common bacterial infection.

When the time comes, many will be forced to load up, aim straight, and bravely fight the undead feeling weak, cold, hungry, thirsty, and suffering from cholera, dysentery, chronic diarrhea, or worse.

If I were a zombie, I'd like those odds.

A FAILING SYSTEM STEPS IN

When the zombie pandemic hits, there will be no vaccine or medical treatment that can help prevent infection. This notion

leads to wild speculation about how individuals and governments will react in the face of a fast-spreading undead threat. But in fact, there is already a clear set of guidelines in place for dealing with similar scenarios, created by organizations such as the U.S. Centers for Disease Control and Prevention.

Nonpharmaceutical intervention (NPI) is what experts call public-health strategies of this type. From mandatory social distancing to quarantine of exposed population, aggressive NPI procedures have been used repeatedly over the past century, starting with the great influenza outbreak of the early 1900s that killed an estimated 100 million people worldwide.

The Texas Department of State Health Services offers an example of the types of measures that will likely be employed.

- Quarantine of the ill and infected at home.
- Quarantine of household members in homes with an ill person.
- Closure of all schools and public buildings.

- Prohibition of social and public gatherings.
- Cancellation of nonessential work responsibilities.
- Relocation of populations to less dense areas.

Though these steps may have little or no impact on the spread of zombieism, it's important to understand what reaction your local, state, and federal authorities will likely have. If not, you run the risk of being escorted from your home by armed soldiers without time to hide, hunker down, or even collect your survival essentials.

Any survival plan should take into account not only the human threat from your fellow desperate citizens but also the threat from wrong and hasty action taken by the very individuals charged with your protection.

Some governors had authorized militias to shoot looters on sight, even though some occasionally joined outposts and were productive.
—Undead Prometheus (2005), Rob Morganbesser

After experiencing the devastation of Hurricane Katrina, Sheriff Larry Deen of Bossier Parish, Louisiana, was determined to get ready for the worst. The *Shreveport Times* reported that Deen recruited 200 men, training them with shotguns, riot shields, batons, and even a .50-caliber machine gun.

Deen said that in the event of a catastrophic event, volunteers would be dispatched to protect vital areas in Bossier from looters or rioters, including grocery stores, gasoline stations, hospitals, and other public meeting places:

We feel if we prepare for the worst, we'll definitely be able to handle the rest.[46]

But is arming hastily deputized civilians and putting them in charge of vital public supplies and services really a good idea? When food is running low and zombies are walking the streets, will these new lawmen look out for the interests of everyone or just those of their own friends and family?

Undoubtedly, giving a select group of people high-powered automatic weapons and a license to kill significantly alters the balance of power in the community. It also assumes that other citizens will readily respect the new authority of their neighbors. Is Bossier Parish in a better position to handle the zombie pandemic than most, or is it even more likely to be plagued by lawlessness and violence because of Sheriff Deen's preparedness measures? Only time will tell.

21: YOUR OWN WORST ENEMY

We've already discussed the likelihood that zombies have a substantially shorter life span than a healthy living person because their rotting bodies sink a little further back into the earth with each passing hour, day, or week. But it turns out that the dead walking the earth means decreased longevity for everyone.

Contributing editor for *Wired* magazine Jonah Lehrer explains that exposure to prolonged stress can substantially shorten a human's life. Stress can cause you to make bad decisions and engage in unnecessarily risky behavior. It can also kill you:

> Numerous studies of human longevity in developed countries have found that psychosocial factors such as stress are the single most important variable in determining the length of a life. It's not that genes and risk factors like smoking don't matter. It's that our levels of stress matter more.[47]

The psychological burden placed on survivors of the coming zombie plague will be as dangerous as any undead horde. If you manage to stay alive through the toughest times, make sure also to stay positive. Your attitude is what will keep you going over the long haul, so you must do whatever it takes to keep your chin up.

Pontypool (2008)

GRANT: Can you tell us what happened? What's happening there, Ken?

KEN: I've seen things today that are going to ruin the rest of my natural life. And I'm scared, I'm scared!

GRANT: Ken, listen to me. It sounds like you're okay where you are, so don't move.

KEN: They're like cannibals and some were naked. They're like dogs. And their eyes, that look!

But a more immediate concern could be psychogenic illness, a phenomenon whereby people experience medical problems despite having no damage to their physical bodies. And I'm not just talking about a mild headache. Vaughan Bell, PhD, explains that symptoms can include paralysis, loss of consciousness, and even blindness:

> They appear in many forms, most spectacularly in what is now diagnosed as conversion disorder, where people can be, to all intents and purposes, blind or paralyzed without having any damage to their eyes or nervous system.[48]

Bell points out that more than 30 percent of neurological patients have symptoms that are only somewhat explained by physical condition. Imagine what that number will be when the dead rise.

Furthermore, psychogenic illness can cause a chain reaction of symptoms that rapidly appear in groups of people. In a zombie plague, this social contagion can leave large swaths of the population unable to defend themselves properly against the undead.

DEATH BY DESPAIR

In the coming zombie plague, panic in the face of extreme stress or delusional thinking when forced to go it alone will likely be a recipe for certain death. But as easy as it is to fall into these and other psychological pitfalls, it can be devastatingly hard to pull yourself out.

Posttraumatic stress sufferer and mental health expert Michele Rosenthal uses her own experiences to warn of just how seductive common trauma disorders can be:

> For a long time, even while I felt controlled, manipulated and devastated by my extreme PTSD symptoms, I wouldn't have given them up, not for anything in the world.[49]

Rosenthal points out that psychologically damaged thinking often makes us feel safe and reinforces our new traumatized view of the world. In other words, illogical actions and dangerous assumptions may seem logical and wise inside the reactive loop of trauma.

To fight this hidden danger, solid preparation and a trusted survival team are essential. It may be impossible to get fully ready for the shock of zombies walking the earth, but the goal should be just to get ready enough to survive.

We can clearly see the damaging effect of trauma in the Chilean mine accident that left thirty-three men underground for months in late 2010. Despite their rousing exuberance after being freed, all but one of the miners have since been diagnosed with severe psychological problems. One miner is building a ten-foot wall around his house, and he can't explain why. Another isn't able to sleep, eat, or even sit in a room with anyone else without being on heavy medication.

In a February 2011 interview, the jovial leader of the miners, Victor Zamora, said that he wishes he were dead because the residual mental and emotional pain is so great.

---

60 Minutes, Episode 44:23 (2011)

ZAMORA: Before I was a happy guy. Now I am having nightmares. I'm having problems. I'm not the same person.

BOB SIMON: What kind of nightmares are you having?

ZAMORA: Being trapped. Watching my friends around me getting killed. Rocks falling. The old me was left to die back in that mine.

There is also a clear connection between chronic despair and prolonged starvation. As acceptable food for human consumption will likely be in short supply when the dead rise, this will be another contributing factor to widespread mental-health issues.

In 1966, the *New England Journal of Medicine* published reports about the linked relationship between starvation and brain damage:

During the early stages of hunger, irritability and emotional lability are the rule, but later profound and continuing apathy occurs. In the most advanced stages of inanition, defects of memory, confusion, hallucinations, delusions, and intellectual deficits become evident.[50]

In addition to having a zombie emergency kit filled with essential gear, maintaining a positive attitude in a catastrophic undead outbreak is just as vital to your survival. Depression and despair already cause negative side effects in tens of millions of people worldwide. In a zombie pandemic, these same mental obstacles will often be the difference between life and death.

This established mental survival kit for wilderness adventure can be easily modified for use in an undead disaster:

1. *Learn and adapt.* As we've seen, anyone who tells you they know exactly how zombies will behave and exactly how to survive them will likely be the first to get eaten. You must be ready and eager to learn from your changing situation and adapt your strategies as needed.
2. *Do what it takes.* When the dead rise, you may have to do things you never imagined, from eating disgusting foods to living in horrid conditions. You need to embrace your new reality unflinchingly and forget about your old home, room, clothes, and other comforts of a world that doesn't exist anymore.
3. *Stay positive.* Nothing will turn out the way you hope in a zombie survival situation. Failure will be the new norm. If you allow negative thoughts to enter the equation, they'll eat your brain faster than any zombie horde, leaving you exposed to mortal danger on all sides.
4. *Visualize success.* No matter what, you must not lose sight of your ultimate objective of establishing a safe and stable life over the long term. Your family and friends may all be gone, but believing in the possibility of a brighter future is the only way to make that future happen.

Ultimately, your survival depends on a combination of luck, circumstance, preparation, and mental ability. If luck and circumstance go your way and you've done what is needed to be physically prepared, don't risk getting killed by zombies or hostile humans because your head's not in the right place.

ONE MISTAKE IS FATAL

Christopher McCandless was twenty-four when he died in rural Alaska. He had safe shelter, fire, and plenty of drinking water. It was the middle of summer, so the dangers of hypothermia did not exist. But he made the single mistake of thinking he was trapped on the wrong side of a raging river, not knowing there was a rope bridge just around the bend.

That error led to another, as it's theorized that McCandless improperly used a book on native plants to scavenge food, not realizing that the poisonous wild sweet pea is easily mistaken for the nutritious wild potato plant. He ate the wrong one, which made him violently ill and eventually led to death by starvation.

In a zombie outbreak, as in many extreme disaster situations, all it takes is one wrong decision to spell certain doom. A single mistake can find you being eaten by an undead horde, attacked and killed by hostile humans, or simply left on your own to perish slowly. Even a sprained ankle can result in deadly complications, meaning that every decision, no matter how small, is life or death. But you won't be the one who makes a silly mistake, because you have a better chance of surviving a zombie outbreak than most, right?

According to several extensive studies done between 1976 and 2002, people have an uncontrollable tendency to believe they are superior to their peers in everything from disaster preparedness to popularity. In fact, this widespread defect in perception even has a name: the Wobegon Effect.

The Wobegon Effect is named after a fictitious town created by radio personality Garrison Keillor, because in Lake Wobegon, "all the women are strong, all the men are good-looking, and all the children are above average." But research psychologist Kim Orleans points out that in reality, at least half of all people are below average in any measurable category. Unfortunately, that's not how we see it:

> *85% of high school students surveyed think they're in the top 50% in ability to get along with others, and 25% of those say they're in the top 1%. What that means is there are a lot of kids feeling a lot more confident about things than they should.*

And this phenomenon doesn't change as we grow older. A recent study of graduate students at Stanford's business school revealed that 87 percent think they're in the top 50 percent of academic performance. Sixty-eight percent of professors at the University of Nebraska believe they are in the top 25 percent of teaching ability. Ninety percent of drivers of all ages say they're safer than average, and 75 percent of senior citizens think they look younger than their fellow seniors.

People across the board think they're less likely than others to have heart disease, get fired, be divorced, or be killed in a natural or man-made disaster. In short, we think we're smarter, tougher, and better prepared than our neighbors.

To combat your own Wobegon Effect in a zombie outbreak, careful preparation is essential. And when you feel that everything is going according to plan, expect the worst just around the next corner.

22: PREPARE OR PERISH

Zombie survival over the longer term requires adjusting to a world without the modern conveniences we take for granted. With no power grid, there is no instant access to heat and light at the flip of a switch. Recharging electronic devices such as phones and radios will prove impossible for many. Those few who have battery- or gas-powered generators will enjoy an advantage for a short period of time, but very soon batteries will die, fuel will become scarce, and the world will be plunged into a darkness it hasn't experienced in hundreds of years.

A promising technology for the coming plague is solar power. Portable solar generators offer a noise-free, maintenance-free alternative designed to last a lifetime. And most can be wheeled to any location, recharging your essential survival gear.

With that said, I'm a firm believer that zombie-survival advice should be practical. Recommendations that don't easily translate to the real world are worthless. And with a price in the thousands and potential cartage concerns if traveling by foot, solar generators aren't right for everyone. But I personally rely on solar as a backup power source, and it has served me well in past times of need.

A visual inspection was made of all the weapons. The solar panels are running efficiently. I dread going on the roof to clean them because I'm sure I'll be spotted. I should do it at night.

—Day by Day Armageddon *(2009), J. L. Bourne*

When it comes to solar power for zombie survival, one small town on the edge of the Mojave Desert has taken a major step toward keeping the lights on when the dead rise. Nipton, California, is almost completely powered by an eighty-kilowatt solar installation, guaranteeing that as the rest of the world is plunged into the dark ages, Nipton will still have all the comforts of modern life.

Nipton's solar power means easy refrigeration, water purification and pumping, tool recharging, weapons manufacturing, and enhanced food production and procurement. Furthermore, the town's isolated location and rugged population of just 250 makes it arguably the most ideal location for zombie survival in the whole United States.

One potential danger facing Nipton is the unwanted attention that electric lights can attract, signaling desperate humans and zombies from great distances in every direction. But the natural defenses of the expansive open landscape and a heavily armed population skilled in wilderness survival suggest that Nipton is an example of the kind of community that will make it through the worst of the coming zombie plague.

DEATH BY SURPRISE

When a 9.0-magnitude earthquake and resulting tsunami hit Japan in March 2011, the Tokyo Electric Power Company had a disaster plan for its Fukushima Daiichi nuclear plant that included one fax machine and a single medical stretcher.[51] Though more than seven thousand local residents worked either directly at the site or in other related operations, there were just fifty safety suits on hand. What resulted was the worst nuclear catastrophe in almost three decades, affecting the surrounding area and national economy worse than the natural disaster itself.

Several months earlier and some eight thousand miles away, millions of people took part in the Great California Shake Out, an event designed to raise awareness about basic disaster-survival skills. Still, while experts guarantee that a massive earthquake will hit the West Coast of the United States in the relatively near future, most residents have done little or nothing to prepare.

Secretary of the California Emergency Management Agency Matthew Bettenhausen said that it's selfish and irresponsible for people not to prepare for the worst, as a large-scale crisis of any type will likely overwhelm the state. Writer and star of *Shaun of the Dead* Simon Pegg echoes Bettenhausen's dire warning, stating that preparation is essential to survival in a zombie outbreak.[52]

When the dead walk the earth, who perishes and who stays alive will largely be determined by how well they prepared before disaster struck. Look around you right now. Do you have the ready tools, skills, and mental fortitude to survive over the long term if civilization collapses this instant? If not, you might want to think about making some changes or risk starving to death, dying of exposure, or being eaten alive by what used to be your best friend.

GET YOUR GEAR

Recommended by disaster experts for use in the aftermath of everything from a devastating hurricane to a large-scale terrorist attack, a seventy-two-hour emergency kit, or bug-out bag (BOB), is a light and portable kit containing all of the essential items needed to survive for three days. When death comes knocking on your door, your BOB is meant to ensure that you don't become a casualty in your own home or have to flee empty-handed.

On May 16, 2011, the U.S. Centers for Disease Control and Prevention (CDC) issued their official zombie outbreak preparedness guidelines, emphasizing the importance of having a well-stocked emergency kit. With a focus on the basics of food, water, and shelter, the CDC lists items that should be included in your BOB:

Water (one gallon per person per day)

Food (stock up on nonperishable items that you eat regularly)

Medications (this includes prescription and non-prescription meds)

Tools and supplies (utility knife, duct tape, battery-powered radio, etc.)

Sanitation and hygiene (household bleach, soap, towels, etc.)

Clothing and bedding (a change of clothes for each family member and blankets)

Important documents (copies of your driver's license, passport, and birth certificate, to name a few)

First-aid supplies (although you're a goner if a zombie
bites you, you can use these supplies to treat basic
cuts and lacerations that you might get during a
tornado or hurricane)

If things get really bad, you may not need your passport or
driver's license anymore. The tent poles of modern civilization, like national border security and traffic laws, may already be out the window. But the CDC list does a good job of
covering the basics.

Other useful items include water purification tablets, a reliable fire starter, and weapons just in case.[53]

Though seventy-two hours of self-sufficiency is thought to
be enough in more common catastrophes, a zombie outbreak
that results in complete societal collapse will likely rule out
the possibility of any rescue within three days, three months,
or even three years. A BOB for zombie survival should therefore hold enough reserves for at least a week, buying enough
time to scavenge for other resources or begin to move from
one safe place to another.

The trick is to strike a balance between your bag's form
and its function. Too much gear packed inside makes it impossible to wear for long periods while accomplishing basic daily
tasks. Too little, and your BOB is rendered useless in many
situations.

Bite Me, Episode 1.4 (2010)

MICHAEL: Oh, man. This is just like *Evil Dead*.

JEFF: This is nothing like *Evil Dead*!

MICHAEL: My God, is this really happening?

JEFF: Listen, the power's out. Did you take the night-vision
goggles?

What's more, a bedroom closet full of weapons, water, and other essentials does little good when zombies attack you at your work across town or swarm your car stuck in rush-hour traffic. You probably don't plan to carry a BOB with you at all times in anticipation of the coming plague, but consider having several stashed in various locations just in case.

Your BOB is there to help save your life, but it can't do its job if it's not within arm's reach.

MAKE YOUR MIND RIGHT

The official psychologist of the Boston Marathon, Dr. Jeffrey Brown, is an expert at treating athletes who are experiencing psychological symptoms related to the extreme stress they put on their bodies and minds. In his book *The Winner's Brain*, Brown interviewed everyone from legendary blues musician B. B. King to trainers at the FBI Academy's firearms division, finding that success is overwhelmingly determined between the ears.

Leif Becker holds multiple world records in martial arts board breaking and couldn't agree more:

Success is determined by an individual's ability to develop the proper emotional state and sustain it while completing various tasks until they achieve their objective. Mental preparation develops clarity, and clarity increases one's certainty in the actions needed to overcome obstacles.

In a marathon, the wrong attitude will find you finishing at the back of the pack. In martial arts, it will cause you to lose a competition or fail to advance to the next belt level. In a zombie plague, the wrong attitude will get you quickly killed and eaten by a mob of ghouls or other hostile humans, and not necessarily in that order.

With this in mind, you might want to consider giving up that morning cup of coffee or daily caffeinated soda, because once the human body becomes dependent on caffeine, an absence of regular infusions can render a person mentally unable to plan and execute any reasonable level of zombie defense.

I saw the effects of caffeine withdrawal firsthand when a former coworker secretly switched her husband's coffee to decaffeinated. The poor guy was in bed for days with a "mysterious" illness. He couldn't eat, couldn't sleep, couldn't concentrate, and certainly couldn't fight zombies. My coworker finally felt so guilty she switched him back to the hard stuff, and his condition instantly improved.

Whatever your guilty pleasure, consider this a warning. The best preparation and planning in the world won't protect you from a zombie attack if you're preoccupied with feeding a habit rather than preventing the undead from feeding on you.

KNOW YOUR ZOMBIES: FIDO

Fido (2006)

Fido, the title character, is an unassuming zombie servant owned by the Robinson family in post-war 1950s America. He serves drinks, plays catch with little Timmy, and seems destined to lead an unassuming death. Of course, things never work out as they're supposed to in zombie movies, even for the zombies.

Fido is a prominent example of the increased humanization of zombies that has emerged in recent years in works like S.G. Browne's novel *Breathers: A Zombie's Lament* (2009) and Comedy Central's animated *Ugly Americans* (2010).

ILLUSTRATION BY CARLA RODRIGUES

23: BUILDING YOUR TEAM

In the 2009 Norwegian zombie romp *Dead Snow*, a group of university students heads off to an isolated mountain cabin for spring break. After a local kook stops by to warn them of potential doom, the gang is attacked by frozen Nazi zombies who stop at nothing to rip them limb from limb.

Despite the fact that they're separated from civilization and can't call for help or easily escape, and despite the fact that they seem unable to defend themselves against their undead attackers, the students have one key survival advantage that you probably won't when facing down your own zombie menace: they are all good friends.

Zombies wait for no one, and they're certainly not going to stand back while you gather your ideal survival team. When it's time to fight for your life, the person by your side is just as likely to be someone you've never seen before as it is an old friend, a coworker, or even a casual acquaintance.

The Walking Dead, Season 1, Episode 5 (2010)

JENNER: Why are you here and what do you want?

GRIMES: A chance.

JENNER: That's asking an awful lot these days.

GRIMES: I know.

JENNER: You all submit to a blood test. That's the price of admission.

What's more, if you do happen to be in a different location from your loved ones when the undead outbreak strikes, it's quite possible that you will never see them again. This harsh reality of zombie survival is often overlooked, but as lines of communication break down and transportation corridors grind to a halt, it's inevitable that many won't make it back home safe and sound.

FEMA's guidelines on emergency readiness suggest that predetermined rendezvous points be established, so a core group of friends and family will know where to find one another:

> *In the event of an emergency, you may become separated from family members. Choose a place to regroup nearby your home. Then choose another location outside of your neighborhood in case you can't return home.*[54]

You may also want to develop a series of protocols that your group can follow. Who is assigned to search for missing members? Who is tasked with staying put in a safe location? If you've ever tried to find someone in a mall with no cell service, you know just how valuable protocols can be.

If all planned efforts to reunite fail, you need to shift focus to your own personal survival and expect your missing companions to do the same. With zombies about, it's not time for a wild-goose chase that's more likely to get you killed than show any tangible results.

NO HONOR AMONG THIEVES

Carlos Marighella was a South American revolutionary who spent his entire adult life developing strategies for small groups to survive under the weight of violent pressure from powerful outside forces. In his book, *The Minimanual of the Urban Guerrilla*, Marighella explains that more dangerous than any external enemy is the enemy that comes from within. He warns of the damage that a person acting in his own self-interest can do when that interest inevitably becomes at odds with the good of the whole.

Ironically, Carlos was killed by police in São Paulo, Brazil, in 1969 after being set up by members of his own movement. But betrayal by members of your group isn't the only deadly pitfall when it comes to working with others.

Imagine you're caught in a catastrophic zombie outbreak. You make it to the edge of the city alone and find refuge at an

 abandoned highway service station. With some food and bottled water taken from the stockroom, you climb to a hidden spot on the roof and try to come up with a plan. Your mind is racing. How did it all fall apart so fast? When will you see your family again? Is this really even happening?

Soon another survivor comes walking up the empty road. It's a woman with her young son. They look tired and desperate, but they're not infected. You make yourself known, share the looted water, and get news of the nightmare unfolding behind you. The zombie horde has grown too large for the military's defenses. They've pulled back to the county line, and the city is lost.

The woman tells you that it's just a matter of minutes before a writhing undead mass makes its way across the blocked entrance ramp, through the piled construction debris, and over the three small hills that lead to you. But there is no reason to run or hide, because she has a plan that is certain to work.

She says that zombies are repelled by the sound of loud music. With her own eyes, she saw a man move straight through a crowd of them holding nothing but a battery-powered radio. She swears it was a miracle, like Moses parting the Red Sea. Another man was hopelessly trapped inside a car, but just as zombies smashed through the windshield, they were suddenly driven back by the blaring dash stereo. She says you have only to turn on the station's speaker system and watch as the approaching menace passes right on by.

You have your doubts, but the speakers are working, and the woman seems so sure of what she saw. What other explanation could there be? Besides, your friends and family are still in the city, and once the threat passes, you can head back to help them. You pull a cheap CD from the revolving rack at the counter, pump up the volume as loud as it will go, and wait.

The horde comes over the hill, slowly marching toward you. They continue within earshot, methodically approaching the station, closer and closer. Soon it becomes clear that the music isn't working. It has no effect. The woman was wrong, but it's too late to run. As you scramble to the roof once more, she reluctantly admits that she heard the story from someone else. But they sounded so sure of what they saw!

Zombies quickly surround you on all sides, pressing against the flimsy structure like a great wave. The speaker system continues to blare as the roof finally collapses, sending you into a mass of biting teeth and pulling hands. You try to fight, but it's no use. You're eaten alive to the echoed sounds of *The Very Best of Dolly Parton, Volume 2.*

Nicholas DiFonzo is professor of psychology at the Rochester Institute of Technology and author of *The Water Cooler Effect*, a study of the power and pervasiveness of false rumors. He writes:

Rumors tend to arise in situations that are ambiguous and/ or pose a threat or potential threat—situations in which meanings are uncertain, questions are unsettled, information is missing, and/or lines of communication are absent.[55]

He concludes that misinformation is fundamental to human nature, and we are all often compelled to believe bad facts and pass them along, especially as part of a group setting. Once you join up with other survivors, you are likely to be swayed by their beliefs and information, even if they're clearly wrong.

SHOULD YOU GO SOLO?

If you can't trust anyone, it's preferable just to go it alone, right? Wrong. In addition to the added time pressures of having to do everything yourself, such as collecting food and water and maintaining safe shelter, the mental stress of isolation is a major obstacle to survival.

The United States is one of the few remaining First World nations that still use solitary confinement to control prison populations, with nearly all other Western countries classifying forced separation as psychological torture worse than any physical abuse. An expert on the mental impact of isolation, Dr. Stuart Grassian, says that people who are alone and confined often become tortured by paranoia.

In a zombie pandemic, you may not be stuck in a single confined space for years on end, but if you choose to go it alone, there will likely be long stretches of isolation. Human beings are social creatures, so prolonged separation from our fellow man can have profound psychological consequences. You may be faster, stronger, and more confident on your own, but you may also lose your marbles.

When forced to go it alone, you can combat loneliness and depression by setting concrete goals and working hard to accomplish them. This type of singular focus not only improves your physical situation, but it also gives you a stable mental platform from which to move forward.

Shock Waves (1977)

ROSE: Chuck, do you feel all right? Chuck, what's the matter?

CHUCK: You've got to let me out of here.

KEITH: Christ. Not now. We can't do it now.

CHUCK: Just let me out. You don't have to come. I can't stay in here any longer!

24: WEAPONS OF WAR

The most effective weapons instruction I ever received was in the French Foreign Legion, the mercenary wing of the French military. But it wasn't what you might think.

One of my trainers, Corporal Blaga, was a short Romanian man with a chip on his shoulder. He hated the fact that he'd been assigned to a teaching unit. And he really hated anyone who was bigger than he, which was pretty much everybody. In my first week, he broke my nose swinging at the burly Russian recruit talking in the mess line in front of me. The Russian ducked, I bled all over my breakfast, and Blaga scurried off as if nothing had happened.

Steven Wieland was a stoic German kid who'd had it rough. Raised by a chronically alcoholic mother and an abusive step-father, Wieland scrounged for basics such as food and clothes growing up. At eighteen, he was six foot two, solid muscle, and my first roommate in the Legion. He didn't drink. He didn't smoke. He didn't lose his temper or even say a bad word about anybody. He was by all accounts a perfect kid who just wanted to keep his head down and go through life unnoticed. Unfortunately, Blaga had other plans.

One night, after a few too many beers and not much else going on around the unit, Blaga decided he needed to assert his authority by making an example of someone, and this time he picked Wieland. He circled us up in a large common room and pulled Steven to the center. After lecturing him incoherently about respect and what it took to be a Legionnaire, Blaga slapped Wieland about the head, getting angrier as the German showed no reaction. Blaga then retrieved a large combat baton from a nearby closet and raised it in the air threateningly. He dared Wieland to attack. He ordered him to charge. But Steven wouldn't move a muscle.

Frustrated, Blaga started to hit Steven with the club, screaming louder and louder. He smacked him in the mouth with its butt end and struck Wieland across the skull and shoulders repeatedly.

With no other options, Steven finally charged, prompting Blaga to deal him one last violent blow to the side of his knee. The German was meant to collapse to the floor in a lump of failure, but instead, Wieland kept coming and delivered a punch to the center of Blaga's face that speckled the room with blood and knocked the Romanian out cold.

I think Wieland was as shocked as the rest of us, and we all just stood there with our mouths open. After what seemed like forever, another trainer came by to see what the silence was all about and quickly carried Blaga to the infirmary. He would later be transferred to a different unit in what was said to be a preapproved move, but we all knew it was because Blaga had lost control of us and we would never take orders from him again.

The next night, a group of seven or eight trainers grabbed Wieland from our room and beat him up pretty good. He came back battered and bruised, but his first words to me in his thick German accent were "Totally worth it."

But what was the Romanian trying to do? He wanted to intimidate us to show that he was in charge, but instead, he got himself reassigned to warehouse duty at the trash yard. Wouldn't a pistol have worked better than a stick for intimidation? Having had both waved in my face at one time or another, I can tell you the answer is a resounding yes.

The lesson I took away is that when given options, it's crucial to pick the right weapon for the job at hand within the range of your abilities. No weapon is the best weapon for everyone or every purpose. My top choice might be last on your list, and rightly so. But ego, testosterone, and fantasy have no place in the decision process if we're talking about actual zombie survival.

USE WHAT YOU HAVE

In a perfect world, your weapons choices would be endless. But after the dead rise, you may not have any options at all.

 With dwindling resources and limited opportunity, your weapon may well be whatever you can scrounge. In *Shaun of the Dead*, it was a cricket bat. In *Dawn of the Dead*, a screwdriver. But you don't have to look to the movies to see that almost any object can represent a deadly threat.

On May 3, 2007, college student Jason Webster murdered a classmate at Hull University in England by stabbing her with a pen. Fifty-seven-year-old widower Jeffrey Burton killed himself with a pencil on September 27, 2009. From bottles to billiard balls, news reports around the world prove time and time again that a weapon is what you make of it.

But no group better illustrates the intersection between ingenuity and armament than the United States prison population. On February 26, 2009, guards at Baraga Maximum Correctional Facility confiscated a knife that was twelve inches long with a six-inch blade and made completely out of toilet paper. Though it had been created in just a few hours with no special materials, the paper shank was rock solid and sharp enough to penetrate a human body easily, highlighting the bitter truth that when there is a strong will to inflict bodily harm and death, there is always a way.

When it comes to firearms for zombie defense, running out of ammunition is often cited as their Achilles heel. A second common knock is that gunshots are loud, revealing your location and inviting countless undead and living dangers. Both are valid points, but there is another much-overlooked flaw that makes your shotgun, rifle, or pistol a potential loser in zombie combat.

Despite what you've experienced in your favorite video game, when you pull the trigger of a firearm in actual combat, chances are you're going to miss your target over and over again.

A study of New York City police officers found that when firing at live targets just nine feet away, their hit rate was a dismal 11 percent. When the target stood at a distance greater than twenty feet, that number dropped to 4 percent, meaning that ninety-six out of one-hundred shots missed their mark. By contrast, these same officers were more than 95 percent accurate when shooting in a controlled gun range. They receive regular training and annual qualifications and are statistically much better shooters than civilians.

When faced with a zombie horde or a gang of roaming human thugs, hearts will race, hands will shake, and bullets will fly everywhere and hit nothing. If you think you're going to be accurate even 15 percent of the time, you're living in a dream world and are likely to wake up to the sound of someone or something chewing your guts out.

> *He kept firing his pistols until they were both empty. Then*
> *he stood on the porch clubbing them with insane blows, los-*
> *ing his mind almost completely when the same ones he'd*
> *shot already came rushing at him again.*
> —I Am Legend *(1954), Richard Matheson*

As we've seen, arguably the most overlooked threat in a zombie outbreak is the human threat. It's one thing to be prepared to take out a member of the undead, but what about someone in your group who goes violently mad? What about a seemingly friendly stranger who later plans to take your food and water, leaving you stranded on the side of the road? Johnny Law isn't going to be around to make sure that justice is served, of that much you can be sure.

My recommendation for nonlethal human threat mitigation is a stun gun. Smaller than a garage door opener and packing upward of a million volts, most come with a lifetime guaranteed lithium battery and an option to buy discounted replacements just in case. Why waste precious ammunition or bludgeon energy when a short burst from your stun gun can incapacitate an attacker for up to ten minutes?

That's plenty of time to get the upper hand or simply get away.

BAD IDEA: SPECIALIZED WEAPONS

Famed samurai warrior Miyamoto Musashi wrote a classic treatise on military strategy called *The Book of Five Rings* in 1645. In it, he emphasizes the need for extensive training to become proficient in the use of weapons.

Musashi compares the traditional Japanese katana to a

musical instrument, suggesting that it's as illogical to believe you can pick up a sword just a few times and then engage in  meaningful combat as it is to believe you can pick up a violin and play beautiful music. But if I had a dollar for every time I've overheard someone with no formal training declare a katana to be the ultimate zombie weapon, I'd be rich by now.

Zombie survival expert Max Brooks says that he doesn't understand the obsession some have with katanas and other weapons of nobility, because they are specifically designed for use by master warriors who do nothing but train all day. He recommends instead a peasant weapon such as the common machete.

In the end, all weapons require practice for one to become truly proficient with them. Specialized weapons just require a lot more practice than most.

So, unless you're a martial-arts enthusiast who gets professional instruction on a regular basis, leave the trophy sword on its fancy black lacquer stand and join the peasant masses like the rest of us. Looking cool is cool, but staying alive is even cooler.

AVOID THE FIGHT

Al V. Corbi is one of the world's leading experts in the field of residential security, having been interviewed on *Oprah*, CNN, MSN, and other major networks and cable news outlets. His own home is widely judged to be the safest house on the planet.

Corbi advises that in a catastrophic survival scenario, combat should never be entered into by choice under any circumstances. Only when all other options are exhausted and your life is in direct and imminent danger should the sword be raised. His reasoning is that no one wins when the situation deteriorates to violence. There are only varying degrees of loss.

And when push does come to shove, it turns out that we're not all natural-born killers. In fact, according to Dave Grossman's seminal work about the psychological cost of taking another person's life, *On Killing*, more than 75 percent of us wouldn't fire a fatal shot at our enemy even if our own lives depended on it.

Grossman observes that the traditional fight-or-flight model is too simplistic when dealing with violence within a single species, and a more accurate breakdown is: fight, flee, posture, or submit·

Piranhas and rattlesnakes will bite anything and everything, but among themselves piranhas fight with raps of their tails, and rattlesnakes wrestle.[56]

With mountains of evidence from past and current military conflicts, *On Killing* proves that it's not a matter of cowardice that makes people passive but an unconscious drive for survival of the species. Soldiers are willing to risk great danger to rescue others, gather supplies, or run messages, but these same men purposefully aim high when firing on the enemy.

Before you discount Grossman's work, citing your phenomenal kill rate in your favorite video game, take note that it is required reading in a wide range of law-enforcement and military institutions in the United States, including the FBI Academy, the DEA Academy, the Air Force Academy, and West Point.

To the extent that our subconscious minds register the

walking dead as another member of the human race, zombie survival isn't going to be nearly as easy as a shotgun and ready ammunition. Even if you're ready to go out with guns blazing, chances are that many others in your group won't fire a single shot.

When the dead rise, consider avoiding combat as if your life depended on it, because in more ways than one, it probably will.

25: TRAVEL AND COMMUNICATION

On Monday, December 10, 2007, Italian truck drivers went on strike, and just two days later, gas stations were sucked dry and food was running out across the country. Citizens did not anticipate the crisis, meaning that there were no long lines at gas stations leading up to the shortage.

When traveling in a zombie world, you can't count on pulling over to a local filling station when your armor-plated Hummer runs short on gas after just a few miles. In fact, even if you have extra fuel, when it comes to fleeing zombies, bigger is not necessarily better. Roads will be clogged with so many other vehicles that driving over or through obstacles will be impossible in anything less than a gas-guzzling tank. Furthermore, road conditions vary so greatly that an off-road-capable SUV may prove utterly worthless.

On a highway overpass, traveling tight city streets, or boxed in by steep drop-offs on a country road, larger vehicles will become immobile cages, fit for speedy abandonment and little else. But even smaller vehicles such as compact cars and motorcycles will prove useless in just a matter of days as fuel runs out across the planet.

We travel light; everything we once owned has now been abandoned, other than crucial items like water bottles, a tin opener, knives and the gun.
—Dead to the World *(2010), Gary McMahon*

HOW AND WHERE TO GO

No matter how well stocked and fortified your zombie shelter, chances are you'll eventually find a compelling reason to hit the road. And with gas a dwindling resource in an undead world, sooner or later, your feet will be what carries you. Along with bringing proper gear and planning well, consider following this travel tip: move at night and off-road.

Summer nights provide a cooler atmosphere for physical activity while eliminating the risk of overexposure to the sun. In moderate climates, night hiking in winter keeps your blood circulating and your core body temperature up. But most important, moving under the cover of darkness allows you to remain undetected by those who would do you harm.

Though slower than mechanized transportation, traveling by foot allows you to adjust more easily to changing terrain, making it an excellent method of stealth movement. A car on an open highway or even a noisy motorcycle along a dirt path is an invitation to every living and undead threat within earshot to seek you out for attack. Even bicycling down the open expanse of a paved road puts an unwanted target on your back.

So when you find yourself surrounded by zombies and on the move, try to stay dark and dirty. Traveling undetected is the best way to avoid lurking dangers and safely make it to your next destination.

Survival of the Dead (2009)

SARGE: Going north we got a better shot at getting closer to
no place.

BOY: We don't want to go no place. We want to go someplace
where this shit can't get at us.

SARGE: Like where?

BOY: Like an island.

One place you don't want to go walking at night is the great white north. In fact, depending on the time of year, you don't even want to go walking during the day. So if your plan is to escape to a place like Alaska when the zombie horde comes, you may want to rethink things completely.

Research physicist and longtime Alaska resident Marcus Mooers has extensive experience with the challenges of Arctic survival. He explains that a single mistake at temperatures  that cold can be fatal in minutes, and the specialized gear needed to withstand extreme northern winters is often not even available in the lower forty-eight states, because there is no market for it.

Logistically speaking, if a zombie outbreak resulted in a large influx of refugees to Alaska and Canada in a matter of weeks, there would be no available shelter to protect them from the cold. Mooers argues that the locals wouldn't necessarily welcome strangers with open arms either:

Supplies here are already limited. With no new infusions of food and medicine, residents are likely to feel protective of the supplies at hand. In fact, new people could wind up not as food for zombies but for other survivors!

He says to play it smart and go south, where you can grow your own food, survive outside, and move about freely. But experienced survivalist and Mojave Desert native Zoe Mora notes that seeking out an isolated survival spot that is too warm can be equally deadly.

Though most people have a basic understanding that deserts are hot and that water is hard to come by, few truly understand how desperate the situation can become. In the summer months, desert creeks are dry, water holes evaporate, and even the few cacti that hold drinking water will be empty. Mora goes on to explain that if you're not fully prepared for the realities of desert survival, you are most certainly going to die:

The desert is harsh and cruel. It's easy to think a 120° weather report on television sounds hot. It's another thing entirely to be out under a blazing sun, with scorching wind literally tearing the moisture from your body so fast you don't even think you're sweating.

Much like in Alaska at night, being active in the summer desert heat can be quickly fatal. Mora says that the only way to survive is to know where you will find your water ahead of time and to have a good map that shows the rivers, canals, and lakes. Short of that, you're toast.

To recap: Cities spell disaster because of their high population density. Heading far north risks a fatal freeze. And the open expanses of desert are deadly. In the unlikely event that you are able to find a workable means of transportation, where should you go? The simple answer is anywhere you can survive with the equipment and abilities you already have.

COMMUNICATION

On July 29, 2008, at 11:42 A.M., there was a minor earthquake in Chino Hills, California, thirty-five miles east of Los Angeles. Though it measured only 5.4 on the Richter scale and caused no damage, cell phones in the greater L.A. area were inoperable for upward of five hours following the shake.

Why? Because millions of people tried to get in touch with their families, friends, and loved ones all at the same time, making it impossible for anyone to connect. Citizens returned to their regular routines within minutes of the quake, but the lines were still so jammed as to render all cell phones completely useless for the better part of the day.

It stands to reason that when zombies begin roaming the streets, cellular phone service will instantly become a thing of the past, a distant memory of more peaceful days gone by. Unless both you and your desired party have predetermined alternative forms of communication—landlines, two-way radios—anyone out of earshot might as well be dead.

So take heed. The terror of being isolated from your fellow man and surrounded by relentless, hungry zombies is not reserved for a lonely rural farmhouse. Faced with the threat of the undead, a city of 12 million can quickly become as desolate and unfamiliar as the dark side of the moon.

Though calls from a cell phone will be impossible during the first hours and days of the coming undead pandemic, bandwidth-friendly text messages may prove invaluable when trying to locate your zombie survival team. That's why CNN contributor Amy Gahran recommends owning a second cell phone to be used in just such an emergency.

But be careful to check battery capacity on the model you choose. Gahran points to the limited battery life of most popular Web-surfing brands as a serious problem in a prolonged disaster. She suggests that a simple backup phone that can hold an extended charge is in order:

> *During Hurricane Katrina, text-messaging saved lives and was a key coordination tool for NOLA.com, according to Online Journalism Review.*[57]

Many discount phones lack the energy-sucking features of your favorite model but can hold their charge for a month, with up to two hundred hours of talking time. For around twenty dollars, it could be the essential tool that saves your life and the lives of your loved ones in an undead crisis.

Gahran also reminds us to program phones with essential zombie-survival numbers before the dead rise, because it's "better to give them a head start early than a head shot later."

The Federal Communications Commission is getting in on the discussion with ten tips for communicating in a major disaster. Here is a breakdown of the FCC recommendations, with comments:

1. *No nonemergency calls.* When your dead neighbor is trying to eat you, what call isn't an emergency?
2. *Keep calls brief.* Sure, it may be the last time you ever talk to your loved ones again, but don't hog the line!
3. *Text-message instead.* When phones are down, texting may be an option for a little while at least.
4. *Wait between calls.* One failed call after another can clog the line, but in a panic, will anyone wait to dial again?

5. *Have charged batteries.* Chances are the power will be out, so your phone will only last as long as a single charge.
6. *Save emergency contacts.* Police, fire, and medical responders will have their hands full, so why call?
7. *Don't talk and drive.* Okay, but I'm not sure if pulling over is the best idea when you're racing through an undead city.
8. *Have a clear plan.* There is no doubt that proper planning and preparation are essential to all aspects of zombie survival.
9. *Forward calls.* You probably won't be home, so the FCC says to forward those calls to your cell. But your cell won't work, either!
10. *Own a corded phone.* This is the best suggestion of the bunch. Old-school dial phones don't require power to work.

In truth, there likely will be no reliable way to communicate by phone in a zombie outbreak. Texting will be only slightly more reliable than calling and won't work when the lines become fully blocked. A rotary landline is great, but unless you're calling someone else with the same setup, you're likely to get an endless busy signal.

Assume that anyone you're not standing next to will be outside your communication zone. Therefore, the only way to ensure that you'll be able to make contact with your group is to establish several primary and secondary meeting points ahead of time.

KNOW YOUR ZOMBIES: NUMBER 9
Land of the Dead (2005)

As planet Earth is overrun by zombies, Fiddler's Green is an enclave protected on three sides by water and on the fourth by armed guards. The rich live in an air-conditioned high-rise and the poor must scrape along the edges of town. But not even this fortified existence is safe from the undead.

Number 9, a girl-next-door softball player gone ghoul, emerges from the water with her bat in hand, alongside a genius gas station attendant zombie who leads an undead insurgency against their violent human oppressors.

ILLUSTRATION BY JOSH TAYLOR

26: WHAT ARE OUR CHANCES?

Because humans are a key ingredient in the creation of zombies, it stands to reason that a higher population density means greater danger in an undead outbreak. That's why new forecasts released by the United Nations show that the human race is setting itself up for certain disaster.

By 2030, 60 percent of the world's population, or 5 billion people, will live inside large urban centers. And 2 billion of those will live in massive shantytowns across Asia and Africa, where new and deadly diseases brought on by unsanitary conditions, malnutrition, and lack of basic health care will run rampant. Huge megacities, rare just a decade ago, will be commonly found all across the planet, as populations cram together in increasingly tight geographic areas.

In terms of zombie survival, we are becoming less self-reliant, less physically and mentally fit, and less able to avoid or escape disaster when it strikes.

Where do you run when the mass of zombies is too thick to penetrate? Where do you hide when your desperate neighbors are so close at hand they can hear you breathing? How do you fight when the undead are less of a threat than the tens of millions of terrified survivors scrambling for life outside your front door?

For too many of us, the answers won't be pretty.

*Whether the defenders had run short of bullets or courage,
I did not know. All I saw were humans in full retreat before
the swarm. Hundreds, perhaps thousands of the creatures
surged over the barricade, crushing their brethren that had
formed a ramp of compressed flesh.*

—The Extinction Parade *(2011), Max Brooks*

CITIES IN PERIL

Experts have long known that population density is a major factor in evaluating a person's risk for falling victim to crime,  disease, and man-made disasters, but it is also the leading indicator of zombie survivability. Overpopulated cities don't just cause problems for urban planners, power suppliers, and pollution regulators; they create a citizenship that is shockingly unable to take care of itself in a crisis.

According to the Population Reference Bureau, before 2000, there were only three urban areas in the world with a population of more than 10 million: Mexico City, New York, and Tokyo. As of 2010, at least thirteen additional cities have reached that size, and in the next ten years, the number of megacities worldwide is expected to double. Add to that another 381 metro areas with a population greater than 1 million, and it's easy to see that the global community is crowding dangerously together.

Despite the traditional cinematic depiction of zombies attacking a small group of survivors in a remote farmhouse, the real danger of a fast-spreading undead sickness lies in big cities. As the trend toward urbanization continues, the world becomes less and less likely to survive the coming zombie pandemic.

In North America, Mexico's big cities are the most tightly packed, but more surprising is Canada's poor showing. Though greater New York City leads the pack in population with 21,295,000, both Toronto and Montreal house more people per square mile. In fact, the three large Canadian urban centers studied—Toronto, Montreal, and Vancouver—beat out an impressive list of fourteen major U.S. cities, including Chicago, Phoenix, Dallas, and Philadelphia.

Even with the best preparations, if your local community becomes a toxic zombie environment, there may be no way to make yourself truly safe. With this in mind, there is a simple way for ordinary citizens to evaluate their own city's chances.

The Regional Outbreak Survivability ranking, or ROS rank, takes into account three primary factors when predicting the level of saturation a zombie outbreak will achieve in any given urban setting:

1. *Combat readiness.* What is the population density in your area? What percentage of the citizenship owns a firearm or has combat training? Are there available military resources stationed nearby?

2. *Infrastructure.* Do the area's roads offer many different travel routes in and out? Is the local climate and topography a strategic advantage? Can abundant freshwater and other resources be easily accessed?

3. *Civil response.* Are police, fire, and rescue services highly trained in emergency preparedness? Is the local population psychologically ready for disaster? Are there ample hospitals and other public services?

Let's use Los Angeles as a test case. The city scores relatively low in combat readiness because of its high population density and average gun-ownership rate. Despite a favorable climate, its infrastructure score is also poor, because transportation options and water resources are horrible. Finally, its civil response score is high because emergency training is excellent, and the threat of earthquakes has created strong cultural preparedness for disaster.

Overall, Los Angeles gets a C+. What is your city's ROS rank?

SURVIVAL ACROSS THE STATES

 By comparing hard statistical data from different regions throughout the United States, including population density, climate, topography, gun-ownership rate, military presence, and public infrastructure, the zombie survival picture becomes clear.

According to the calculations, the Northeast rates lowest in likely survivability against the undead. Eight of the top ten states in terms of population density are in that region, with New Jersey leading the pack at one thousand people per square mile. But the supporting data don't stop there.

The Northeast also has extremely low gun-ownership rates, with six of the least-armed states being in that area of the country. A lot of people and not a lot of firearms, along with crowded urban centers and clogged transportation corridors, lay the groundwork for a deadly explosion in the zombie population.

Which region is the safest? The middle Northwest boasts low population density and high gun ownership, with Idaho, Montana, Wyoming, South Dakota, and North Dakota landing in the top ten in both categories. In fact, Wyoming is rated second highest in overall survivability, with just five people per square mile and topping the list with an estimated gun-ownership rate of almost 65 percent. The region benefits from rugged terrain accented by large expanses of open land and an impressively self-reliant population.

Standing out above the rest, Alaska captured the top spot. Though it came in second in combat readiness, it boasts only one person per square mile. But as we've seen, Alaska's natural benefits offer specific challenges, too, highlighting the fact that no place is perfect when it comes to zombie survival.

TOP TEN STATES
1. Alaska
2. Wyoming
3. Montana
4. South Dakota
5. Idaho
6. North Dakota
7. Arkansas
0. Utah
9. West Virginia
10. Mississippi

BOTTOM TEN STATES
41. California
42. Delaware
43. Florida
44. Illinois
45. Maryland
46. New York
47. Connecticut
48. Massachusetts

49. Rhode Island
50. New Jersey

To be clear, living in a state at the bottom of the survivability list doesn't guarantee certain doom any more than living in one at the top guarantees success. I would much prefer to be fully emotionally and physically ready for a zombie outbreak in Massachusetts than caught completely off-guard and unprepared in Montana. Ultimately, true zombie survival is an individual concern, with each person making the choices necessary to either stay alive or die trying.

Ratings and statistics are important only to the extent that they give you a better understanding of the bigger picture, providing insight into potential areas of concern in your survival landscape.

27: THE GLOBAL VIEW

According to the American Red Cross's 2010 World Disasters Report, the next global disaster—whether natural, man-made, or zombie—may well be even worse than any we've experienced in the past several decades. The report finds that rapid urbanization, poor local governance, population growth, inadequate health services, and a rising tide of urban violence make the human race increasingly vulnerable to catastrophe.

Daniel W. Drezner, professor of international politics at the Fletcher School of Law and Diplomacy at Tufts University, has done extensive research on likely governmental reactions to a global zombie plague. His resulting nonfiction work, *Theories of International Politics and Zombies,* was published by Princeton University Press in February 2011.

Drezner argues that preventing an undead outbreak isn't possible, because we don't know how zombies will ultimately be created and where they will first crop up. The only option is contingency planning for a worst-case scenario, but as we've seen with any number of other large-scale disasters in recent years, that planning is rarely done:

> *It's a global reality. Governments are composed of bu-*
> *reaucracies, and what all bureaucracies try to do is create*
> *standard operating procedures to handle routine things.*
> *Zombies aren't routine, and applying these procedures to*
> *them likely won't work very well.*

Overwhelming evidence suggests that bureaucracies will fal-
ter in the face of a zombie pandemic, but what of the world's
military establishment? Couldn't the stronger nations overpower their undead foe with strict discipline and overwhelming firepower? Or at the very least, wouldn't the threat of
human-on-human violence be quelled by the mere presence
of government troops?

As we have seen, when disaster strikes hardest, abundant
food and potable water jump to the top of the list of survival
priorities. Without water to drink, you can't make it more
than a week. Without food, you've got a month, tops. This
immediate need for the essentials of life has the potential to
undermine any military effort to control the worsening situation. And because zombies don't share the same survival
limitations, they continue to multiply and grow stronger in
numbers, while the global population grows weaker by the
day.

In the weeks after the devastating Haitian earthquake of
2010, upward of fifteen thousand U.S. troops were sent to
keep the peace, with their primary objective being to protect
the precious relief supplies arriving from all over the world.
With a total Haitian population of just 9 million, that's roughly
one soldier for every six hundred people. Still, reports of violence and looting were rampant.

To reach that same level of military presence within the
United States, the government would need to deploy 517,000

troops to the streets of every city and town from Florida to Oregon. That's roughly 90 percent of the active-duty soldiers in the entire army assigned to protect pallets of bottled water. And if a zombie outbreak causes desertion rates to spike, the other branches of service could be swallowed up, too. Would you show up for duty in Georgia knowing your spouse and children might be attacked and killed in your home in Iowa?

No doubt, some nations will fare better than others, simply because of their military capability, infrastructure, and stocked resources. So, which is the best, and which is a zombie nightmare waiting to happen?

THE WORLD'S WORST

When comparing the outcomes of a zombie outbreak with other more common natural and man-made disasters, we find that the worst places to be are generally poorer countries with dense populations. Authoritarian regimes often fail miserably under the weight of these large-scale stresses, too. Which countries rank lowest globally in the case of a catastrophic undead pandemic? All available data clearly point to two that are likely doomed.

With 1.35 billion people living on 3.7 million square miles of land, China has a population density lower than that of Connecticut, Rhode Island, Massachusetts, and New Jersey. However, its paltry gun-ownership rate of just 3.5 percent means that the People's Republic has a fraction of the number of armed citizens residing in the United States. Add into the mix a notoriously secretive government that rules with an iron fist, and China ranks near the bottom in global zombie survivability. But another country is even worse off.

Without a doubt, India is the last place you want to be in a zombie pandemic. It packs in 944 people per square mile, making it an ideal recruiting ground for new undead conscripts, and of a total population of 1.3 billion, less than 4 percent own firearms. Furthermore, India's military is substantially smaller and not as well equipped as that of either China or the United States.

Dead Snow (2009)

VEGARD: She's not here right now. She's skiing across the mountains.

OLD MAN: Skiing across the mountains?

LIV: She's a bit sportier than the rest of us.

VEGARD: Why? Is the terrain dangerous?

OLD MAN: The terrain is the least of your worries up there.

BEST COUNTRIES

We've seen the worst, but where is the best? At first glance, countries with remote or hard-to-traverse terrain tend to stand out. Other desirable attributes include ample food supplies, a self-reliant population, and solid military and civilian defense capabilities.

Note that only nations with a population of more than 5 million were included in this evaluation. So a country like New Zealand, with a citizenship of just 4.4 million, did not meet the criteria for consideration.

Here is a list of the top ten safest countries in a zombie outbreak:

10. *Sweden.* A favorably small population and many natural defenses help Sweden capture the tenth spot. Its military is well trained, well equipped, and solely focused on the defense of its people and lands.

9. *Argentina.* As the eighth-largest country in the world by landmass, Argentina is sandwiched by the Andes Mountains and the Atlantic Ocean. Its high level of urbanization keeps it from climbing higher on the list.

8. *Finland.* The Finnish benefit from being surrounded by other countries strong in zombie survivability, and their population density of just forty-one people per square mile doesn't hurt, either.

7. *Norway.* The fact that the tiny country of Norway came in second in gold medals at the 2010 Winter Olympics shows that Norwegians know how to thrive in icy conditions. A lot of snowy land and a few hearty people to defend it is a recipe for survival.

6. *Bolivia.* With mountains to protect the population from its neighbors and the worst economy in South America, Bolivians are adept at managing without modern conveniences and can ably fend for themselves.

5. *Kazakhstan.* Borat made the whole world laugh at this little country, but Kazakhstan may get the last laugh. The rugged terrain, formidable climate, and extremely low population density are key survival factors.

4. *Russia.* Low population density, huge land barriers, and a battle-tested people give Russia the number four spot. If the Nazis couldn't take Leningrad, there's no reason to think that zombies will.

3. *United States.* With more than eighty-three people per square mile, the United States is considerably more dense than any other country in the top five, but its

heavily armed citizenship is more ready for a battle than most.

2. *Canada.* Sure, its 35 million residents are packed in a thin strip along the country's southern border, but gun ownership is common, and there's plenty of room to head north when the dead rise.

1. *Australia.* This vast nation grabs the top spot because of its population density of just 7.5 people per square mile and the fact that it has the world's biggest moat surrounding it on all sides.

As we've seen, traveling even a short distance in an undead world will be a dangerous and slow affair. Building your survival plan around simply hopping on a plane to the Aussie outback at the first sign of the zombie plague is extremely ill-advised. No matter how high on the list, a given country is only suitable for extreme survival to its own population or those few outsiders who are intimately familiar with the climate, culture, and resources.

Running off to some perfect new land that will welcome you with open arms and readily provide everything you need to thrive is a fairy tale, and when the dead walk, fairy tales get you killed.

28: PAST OUTBREAKS

In the winter of 1918, history's most lethal virus was born in an army camp in Kansas, then quickly spread, killing as many as 100 million people worldwide in little more than a year. In terms of the panic it caused and the lives it destroyed, the Spanish flu is the closest thing to a trial run for a global zombie pandemic that the modern world has ever seen.

The Department of the Navy's records for that period give a glimpse into the collateral problems generated by so many dead so quickly:

> Bodies started piling up in the road. In a vision not seen since the Black Death of medieval Europe, carts went through the streets, their drivers calling for people to bring out the dead for burial. Wagon loads of bodies were buried together, some having died weeks earlier. Highway workers dug large trenches and filled them to capacity.[58]

If zombies carry with them the same disease and filth as a human corpse—and there is no reason to think they don't—one of their greatest weapons might be their ability to spread sickness from afar.

A handful of bodies left out to rot in the elements can generate a putrid smell for some distance, but hundreds of thousands of rotting bodies could literally create a toxic death-cloud that invades the lungs of hiding humans, rendering them too sick to defend themselves before a single ghoul is even in the same zip code.

Imagine coming down with a high fever. Your head is pounding, you're sweating bullets, you can hardly see straight, and the thought of eating makes you physically ill. After three or four days of this, there's finally a scratching at your front door. By the time zombies come to finish off what's left of you, death seems like a welcome change, as you're too weak even to fight back.

We'd seen these things on TV, but to be this close was something else. I wanted to take a deep breath to settle my nerves, but the stench made that seem like a bad idea.

—Groundwood *(2010)*, Bev Vincent

No scent is more distinctive and revolting than that of death. The stench is so universally repugnant that even insects avoid coming in contact with the dead of their own species. In 2009, biologist David Rollo of McMaster University in Canada made this discovery accidentally while researching the social behavior of cockroaches. Rollo found that when he crushed dead cockroaches, spreading their body juice across a specific area, other roaches wouldn't dare come near:

It was amazing to find that the cockroaches avoided places treated with these extracts like the plague. Naturally, we wanted to identify what chemical was making them all go away.[59]

Though human noses can't easily detect the fatty acids of dead bugs, we are repelled by the sickly-sweet smell of mammalian corpses, especially those other humans. Anyone who has smelled even a tiny dead mouse under the stairs will never forget the stench of death.

There's a lot we can learn from past outbreaks of other more common deadly pandemics, but what of zombie outbreaks throughout history? There are no confirmed incidents in the historic record, but by investigating possible attacks from the past, we can hope to reach a better understanding of the threat we may soon face.

ZOMBIE COLONY OF ROANOKE

In 1587, the colony of Roanoke was established on a small island along the coast of present-day North Carolina. One hundred fifteen men and women eagerly arrived at what they thought would become the first permanent English settlement in the New World. The group was well stocked with supplies and lived in secure structures that offered good protection from the elements and any unfriendly neighbors.

The mystery of Roanoke began when a supply ship returned in 1590 to find not a single living soul and no evidence of war, famine, or any other possible reason for the colony's complete disappearance. In fact, there is still no generally accepted explanation for what happened to those settlers, leading some to suggest that it may have been the work of zombies.

Max Brooks included a fictional zombie outbreak on Roanoke in his 2003 bestseller, *Zombie Survival Guide*, and now it seems life is imitating art, as noted Harvard archaeologist Lawrence Stager recently unearthed evidence of mass cannibalism at the Roanoke site.[60]

No doubt, a sudden undead plague sweeping through the unprepared colony would quickly become a horrific, violent feast, leaving not a single man, woman, or child alive. The relative isolation of the settlement and the time elapsed before the return of the supply ship might have allowed for the remaining colonial zombies to rot back into the earth. Without any humans left to feed on and therefore no way to spread the infection, the zombies would have simply died off.

If the colonists did experience a catastrophic undead event, there could be something sinister still in the ground on Roanoke Island, waiting to be released into a modern population that is more advanced, more connected, but just as unprepared as ever.

What's more, if the settlers on Roanoke Island were, in fact, overrun by a deadly zombie outbreak, then there are certain important date markers to note. They landed at their new home on July 27, 1587, and exactly one month later, the ships that delivered them sailed back to England. Then, on August 18, 1590, the ships returned to bring supplies and support to the new colony, but they found not a single living soul.

Even if the Roanoke zombie plague began just days after the ships sailed, the lack of human remains found upon their return indicates that an outside estimate for the zombie life span would be two years. It could obviously be much shorter, but two years is a probable max.

The notion is that there must have been enough time for zombies to completely overrun the colony, leaving no one left alive, and then wander the island aimlessly until they slowly decayed back into the earth. By the time the reinforcements arrived, there would be nothing for them to discover.

ROME IN RUINS

In March 2010, archaeologists excavating ancient Roman ruins in Italy uncovered a mysterious lead coffin weighing almost a  thousand pounds. Not only is the metal slab bizarrely heavy, but it's also folded over its encased corpse like a "burrito."

Some baffled experts speculate that a notable figure from the third century must have been given the rare honor of a sheet-metal burial, but others speculate that the coffin was meant not as an honor but to keep the dead man from getting out.

Managing director of the project Jeffrey Becker cautions about making any assumptions about the mysterious remains:

> *All we can say so far about the contents is that the lead wrapping contains a human skeleton—or at least a portion thereof—as there is visible bone at the open, foot-end of the sarcophagus.*[61]

What makes the discovery all the more bizarre is that Romans were not normally buried in coffins at all, and when they were, the coffins were always wooden. And because the Romans didn't embalm their dead, instead burying the washed body in a shallow grave, it stands to reason that a zombie from that era would have no trouble clawing back to the surface.

Clearly, there is no evidence of a widespread zombie outbreak in ancient Rome, but if a traveling warrior or nobleman did return home with an unknown sickness that caused him to die slowly and then rise from his grave, this mysterious lead casket just may have been the practical solution for his terrified family.

At this point there were daily reports all over the news about the horrific wounds our soldiers were suffering. Some images had also been leaked online: bodies torn to pieces, sometimes barely anything left for a family to bury.
—The Zombie Combat Manual *(2010), Roger Ma*

Several months later and fourteen hundred miles away, a second team of archaeologists discovered an ancient Roman mass-grave site in York, England, that dates back to the first century. Eighty skeletons were found showing signs of extremely violent injury and decapitation. Could zombies be to blame?

Though some experts claim this must be a gladiator cemetery, lead investigator Kurt Hunter-Mann cautions against hasty assumptions, explaining that they have no conclusive understanding of what they've unearthed:

At present our lead theory is that many of these skeletons are those of Roman gladiators. But the research is continuing and we must therefore keep an open mind.[62]

Roman amphitheaters are known to have existed in several settlements across England, but no evidence of a gladiator arena has ever been discovered in York, which has forced researchers to fall back on the notion that it must be a graveyard for soldiers. But the high number of decapitations undermines this theory.

If this finding is the end result of an ancient zombie outbreak in England, the battle wounds and headless corpses could be easily explained.

UNDEAD IN THE AMERICAS

The primitive Jivaro people of the Ecuadorian Amazon are one of many headhunting cultures found throughout history, but what set them apart was their singular practice of carefully collecting each head they removed, then boiling it in a scalding pot of water for up to three weeks.

This process created tiny shrunken heads, an oddity made famous by explorers at the turn of the last century. But even stranger is the Jivaro's reason for going through such trouble. They claimed their ancestors had faced a great demonic menace many hundreds of years before, and each generation was obligated to continue the practice or risk total tribal extinction.

Is it possible that the tradition dates back to a time of conquest, in which the Jivaro came across a tribe already consumed by some undead plague? Death by decapitation would not work in that case, as detached zombie heads would continue to look around and gnash their teeth, much to the horror of the Jivaro, no doubt.

The extreme ritual of sewing the eyes and mouth shut before boiling the disembodied head would then be a logical step to take when faced with such a bizarre and ungodly enemy as a primitive zombie horde. Furthermore, cooking the brain until it became a worthless pile of mush would no doubt be an effective way to ensure that any remaining life force was removed.

Because the Jivaro were known for their ferocity in battle, they would likely have been able to overcome the zombie threat they faced so long ago. But if they did, in fact, face an undead horde, the fight left a permanent mark on the tribe, as evidenced by the tradition of head shrinking and the dire warning passed on from one generation to the next.

Dead Meat (2004)

ELENA: Do you know how many have been infected?

BAZEL: I'm not sure. Must be spreading quickly, though. I came
across four or five of them before I ran into you. I'm
Bazel, by the way.

ELENA: Elena.

BAZEL: I'm the local grave digger.

Moving north, we look to one of the most advanced tribes in the early Americas, the Anasazi of Chaco Canyon, New Mexico. They thrived for hundreds of years in the fertile red desert canyons, growing their culture and building impressive ancient villages. But at the end of the thirteenth century, the Chaco Canyon people mysteriously and permanently disappeared. Though no universally accepted reason for this sudden decline has been found, recent archaeological discoveries have led to the suggestion that a zombie plague may have been at work.

In 1997, a large quantity of Anasazi human remains were uncovered that showed evidence of death by violent dismemberment and cannibalism. Other excavations of sites from that same area have revealed many more unburied, dismembered, and partially eaten bodies. These findings are particularly disturbing because there is nothing in the Anasazi tradition to explain why a peaceful people would resort to eating other human beings while they were still alive. Furthermore, the possible explanations of war and famine have been largely ruled out by experts.

If cultures as disparate as the ancient Roman Empire and warrior tribes of Ecuador may have experienced their own infestations of the undead, could the mystery at Chaco Canyon be just another reminder of the fragility of civilization in the face of an overpowering zombie threat?

SECTION IV

POPULAR CULTURE

On the second weekend of March 2011, the Far West Popular and American Culture Association held its twenty-third annual convention at the Palace Hotel and Casino in Las Vegas. Presentation topics included the influence of photography in Civil War–era newspapers, the portrayal of homosexuality on cable television, and the rhetorical, linguistic, and political relevance of rapper Lil Wayne. But the star of the event was unquestionably the modern zombie.

In his ninety-minute keynote address, Professor H. Peter Steeves of DePaul University discussed the meaning of zombies in contemporary culture, with references to everything from Freudian theory to Pinocchio. He concluded that not only are zombies a cultural juggernaut, but it's entirely likely that they will someday replace the human race when natural selection finally passes us over. As Steeves put it:

You may think that this is all rather depressing, and it is. But sometimes the point is not that it is all going to end. Sometimes it's about how *it all ends.*

At that very moment, actors dressed as rotting zombies invaded the ballroom, stalking the crowd of scholars and academics and attacking a planted audience member who promptly changed into a flesh eater himself. Steeves threw on a replica of Michael Jackson's famed red leather jacket, and the zombies joined him onstage for an extended dance routine to the sound of Jackson's "Thriller."

Thriller, released in 1982, is the bestselling album of all time, and the companion video for its title song is arguably the most iconic ever made. It features a voice-over by horror legend Vincent Price and dancing zombies that rise from the grave "to terrorize your neighborhood." "Thriller" is the only music video preserved in the Library of Congress's National Film Registry as a cultural, historical, and artistic treasure. It's been decades since Jackson first taught zombies to dance, and they still haven't stopped.

In 2007, corrections officers at the remote maximum-security Filipino prison in Cebu videotaped 1,500 inmates gy-rating in an exact restaging of the famous "Thriller" dance. Posted online, the video has had upwards of 100 million views and was featured in *Time* magazine as one of the most popular viral videos ever.

That same year, Thrill the World was launched as an annual free event in which dancers from across the globe simulta-neously perform Jackson's zombie dance. Today hundreds of different venues in dozens of countries participate, with the numbers growing each year. In 2009, Guinness World Records certified the largest "Thriller" dance to date when nearly 14,000 university students dressed as zombies and lurched around Mexico City's Plaza de la República.

Despite these massive outbreaks of zombie popular cul-ture and nearly fifty years of cultural relevance and com-mercial success, the mainstreaming of zombies in recent years has many suggesting that they're just a fad doomed to fade. Scott Kenemore, bestselling author and zombie expert, couldn't disagree more, saying that what some characterize as a current craze is actually just the modern zombie ascending to its appropriate place in our cultural landscape:

Vampires are everywhere. But people forget that Dracula *was written in 1897. It's had over 100 years to percolate into our books, movies, and media. Zombies haven't had as much time to fully seep into the culture, but I think that's just what we're seeing right now.*

The power of the modern zombie lies in its ability to rise within a population, spreading and infecting new people and leading to eventual domination of the species. Like the dancing hordes that continue to spring up in greater numbers online and across the blogosphere, one zombie invariably leads to two, then ten, then ten thousand. This is key in their dramatic representation onstage, on-screen, and in print and is also a fundamental reason for their popularity at the grassroots level.

Zombies are here, they're hungry, and they're not going away—certainly not from popular culture, anyway.

KNOW YOUR ZOMBIES: MICHAEL JACKSON
Thriller (1983)

Michael Jackson is arguably the most famous zombie of all time. In his video "Thriller," a young couple on a date goes to the movie theater to be scared by fictional werewolves. The real horror awaits them outside as the dead rise on their walk home.

Before his death in 2009, Michael Jackson made dozens of wildly popular music videos, but none as iconic as "Thriller."

ILLUSTRATION BY ALEX GALLEGO

29: WHY ARE ZOMBIES SO POPULAR?

Legions of fans across the globe believe that there is almost nothing that can't be made more fun, more frightening, or more socially relevant by adding zombies, and in most cases, they're right. But what is it about the undead that has so many of us endlessly clamoring for more? Why are they so popular?

Robert Kirkman is the creator of *The Walking Dead*, a long-running graphic novel turned critically acclaimed cable television drama about a ragtag band of survivors struggling to find their way in a zombie infested world. The series broke ratings records in its first season, making Kirkman an established figure in contemporary zombie culture. I sat down with him to talk shop. Here's what he had to say about increasing interest in all things zombie in recent years:

> *People come up to me all the time to say they love the show even though they weren't zombie fans before. But* The Walking Dead *isn't about the zombies, it's about people. It's about us. It's about how we respond to crisis. And that's the case with any good zombie story. So I tell them they actually were zombie fans before; they just didn't know it yet.*

Certainly, the immense popularity of zombies is partly a result of the uncertain times in which we live. Terrorist attacks, economic meltdowns, and environmental calamities dominate the headlines. New and deadly diseases are evolving at an alarming rate, prompting even the most stoic of experts to warn of potential doom. Disaster seems a foregone conclusion. It's not a matter of if, but of when and where.

But it's not just that a zombie pandemic seems to speak to our anxieties about the tragedies and destruction we see in the world around us. Many argue that zombies ring true because they *are* us. They are nothing more than the personification of our own failings come back from the dead to eat us out of existence before we screw things up any more than we have already. Writer and philosopher Ayn Rand famously observed that modern man is an abject zombie on a forced march through a meaningless life, and she may have a point.

For the first time in human history, more of the world's population lives in crowded urban centers than rural environments, and in most industrialized nations, that number is quickly approaching 90 percent. Correspondingly, global job satisfaction is at its lowest point in more than two decades,[63] with the younger generations leading the pack in unhappiness. We grow up. We get uninspiring jobs to pay the rent. We work our whole lives to no real end. We get promotions. We get laid off. We find new uninspiring jobs that are pretty much the same as the old ones. We sit in traffic and wonder how it came to this. We grow old. Our health fails. We die. Another zombie bites the dust.

Before becoming one of the most influential authors of the twentieth century, Franz Kafka had a career as a corporate lawyer at an insurance agency in Prague. He hated everything about it, stating that office work should not be considered a proper occupation but, rather, a form of decomposition:

What do I do? I sit in an office. It is a foul-smelling factory of pain, in which there is no sense of happiness. And so I quite calmly lie to those who inquire after my health, instead of turning away like a condemned man—which is in fact what I am.[64]

I hope your job doesn't stink as badly as Kafka's did, but as a veteran of the corporate grind myself, I certainly know where he's coming from.

Another contributing factor to the modern zombie's current relevance is that it has no long-standing literary tradition. In fact, the last dozen years aside, zombies have almost no literary tradition at all. Unlike most other popular monsters, zombies don't reflect the ancient superstitions of a bygone age. They're not born of myth or legend. There is no romance in the living dead, no classic hero or moral lesson to counterbalance their grinding advance. They aren't driven by religious commitment, lost love, or some misguided yet noble pursuit. Their curse can't be cured by a battle victory, a kiss, or a kind word. They are the here and now. They are the painful reality of what we must suffer in this life. Simply put, they are the most compelling, relevant, and enduring monster of the last half century.

And they happen to scare the bejesus out of me.

The Simpsons, Episode 17:2 (2005)

BART: Your screams when zombies chomp your brains will warn me so I can get away.

LISA: There's no such thing as zombies.

BART: Glad to hear you say that, because the person who doesn't believe in zombies is always the first to get feasted upon.

LISA: Stop scaring me!

30: AT THE MOVIES

D ollar for dollar, horror is the most popular and profitable film genre, with its comparatively low production costs and obsessively loyal fan base. It's also, unfortunately, the least respected. Dozens of celebrated actors got their start in successful horror franchises, including Johnny Depp in *A Nightmare on Elm Street* (1984), Jennifer Aniston in *Leprechaun* (1993), and Kevin Bacon in *Friday the 13th* (1980). But horror movies themselves are routinely dismissed by critics and ignored during awards season. And the least respected subgenre in horror, deep at the bottom of the barrel, is unquestionably the zombie movie. Even comedy legend Rodney Dangerfield, who made a fortune out of being the butt of his own jokes, recognized the lowliness of zombies. As he riffs in one of his routines:

> *I walked into a bar and asked the bartender to make me a zombie. He took one look and said, "God beat me to it!"*

In March 2010, the eighty-second Academy Awards ran a three-minute video tribute to modern horror in film. Zombies were featured on-screen for less than one second. It was a flash so brief that if you blinked, you'd miss it. Other movies receiving considerably more time in the tribute were the 1988 comedy *Beetlejuice*, the Steve Martin musical *Little Shop of*

Horrors, and the romantic teen juggernaut *Twilight*. None of these is actually a horror movie, underscoring the widespread confusion that exists about what horror is, even within the governing body of the industry.

If horror is confusing, then zombies are a complete mystery. While other film monsters enjoy clearly defined characteristics and widespread acceptance, the modern zombie continues to languish in the shadows while scholars and film critics make sweeping statements about the living dead that don't hold up to the harsh light of reality. In fact, scholars and critics who write about zombie films often include a wide range of horror, comedy, and action movies in their zombie category, despite the fact that no actual zombies are ever featured on-screen. This irresponsible cataloging does the subgenre a great disservice and literally drives me insane.

NIGHT'S INFLUENCE

I recently rewatched *Night of the Living Dead* with my twelve-year-old nephew. He'd never seen it before, so I explained to him that each zombie movie has a specific set of rules for its undead creatures to follow. Some are afraid of fire. Some are slow and lumbering. Some can open doors and use tools. Some can even speak. He thought about this for a few minutes and then jokingly asked, "Is one of the rules in this movie that the zombies have to stay twenty feet away from the camera?"

Insulting *Night* is fighting words in my book, no matter how old you are. But in my nephew's defense, he was referring to repeated wide shots of zombies milling about outside an isolated farmhouse while survivors inside argue over what to do to stay alive. I had to remind myself that because he's grown up on contemporary zombie video games and movies, the notion of the dead rising to eat the living is nothing new to him. But when *Night of the Living Dead* was first released on an unsuspecting public in the late 1960s, it scared the wits out of just about everybody, including some of the biggest names in modern horror.

Legendary author Stephen King was a junior in college when the film premiered, and he has said that it turned him to jelly. Director of the *Evil Dead* and *Spider-Man* franchises Sam Raimi credits *Night of the Living Dead* as being the first film to have a profound impact on him:

> *I was probably about ten years old and my sister snuck me into the theater under her coat, if you can believe that. It was a crime that she committed against me, watching that film. I was too young. And it blew my mind, the terror. I could not believe it. I was so terrified watching that film.*[65]

In his late twenties, Wes Craven had never seen a horror movie before and had no interest in the genre. A friend dragged him to Romero's *Night*, and it shook him to the core: "I was hooked, and it was George's fault."[66] Craven would later go on to direct dozens of iconic modern horror films, including *The Hills Have Eyes, A Nightmare on Elm Street*, and the wildly popular *Scream* franchise, to name a few.

ZOMBIE MOVIE HIGHLIGHTS

As we've seen, George Romero quite literally invented the modern zombie with his 1968 classic, *Night of the Living Dead*. Since then, hundreds, if not thousands or tens of thousands, of zombie films and videos have been made by backyard filmmakers and big-name directors in the United States and elsewhere, taking Romero's flesh eater in new and creepy directions. Though covering them all would require a book in itself, here are a few highlights of some important historical moments in zombie movie history, post-*Night*.

ZOMBIE (1979)

In 1979, the late Italian horror director Lucio Fulci released *Zombie*. Fulci is widely referred to as the Godfather of Gore, and he didn't hold back in this film. Italian zombie movies are known to be more bloody and gross than their American counterparts. In keeping with this reputation, *Zombie* includes tight shots of a woman getting her eye gruesomely poked out with a stick.

But the most famous scene in the film follows a topless female scuba diver as she's threatened by a shark until a zombie emerges from an underwater reef to attack her as well. The zombie then does battle with the shark, which rips off the zombie's arm and swims away after suffering a bite. In zombie circles, this scene is so famous that it has led to people using the name "Zombie vs. Shark" for everything from Web sites to rock bands. A clip of the scene was also featured in a 2010 national television ad for Windows 7, Microsoft's new operating system. Dozens of Italian zombie splatterfests would follow in the eighties and nineties, but Fulci's *Zombie* is the film that kicked off the "spaghetti undead" craze.

RETURN OF THE LIVING DEAD (1985)

In 1985, writer-director Dan O'Bannon's *Return of the Living Dead* premiered to mixed reviews and midlevel success, but it has since become arguably the second-most influential film in zombie culture behind Romero's *Night of the Living Dead*.

O'Bannon's film takes Romero's theme and moves it into spoof territory, as a pair of bumbling medical-supply workers accidentally release a secret government toxin on a bunch of cadavers in their warehouse. The cadavers start jumping around, so the workers cut them up and burn the evidence, sending infected smoke out the chimney and into the atmosphere. Enter a rainstorm.

Ashes soon fall back to earth, making the dead in the nearby cemetery rise from their graves and seek out living humans. But instead of eating human flesh, the zombies in *Return* only want brains. This was the first time in film history that any zombie had eaten brains, said "brains," or expressed any interest in brains at all. Today the *Return of the Living Dead* franchise remains the only major film series to include zombies that eat brains. Nevertheless, at every zombie walk and at other zombie-themed events, you will see people chanting that they want brains. This illogically comical notion caught on and will now forever be associated with the modern zombie. We have O'Bannon to thank for that.

RAIDERS OF THE LIVING DEAD (1986)

It's hard for me to name the worst zombie movie of all time. Ultimately, that's a question of personal taste. But one year after *Return of the Living Dead* premiered, a film that's on my short list was released: *Raiders of the Living Dead* (1986). Starring Scott Schwartz of *The Toy* and featuring homemade laser guns and public-domain Three Stooges footage, this stinker follows the confused investigations of a hack reporter and his accidental teen sidekick as they try to figure out why dead bodies are roaming their quiet suburban neighborhood. But even that basic description gives the haphazard events that unfold on-screen too much credit. With a poster stolen from *Star Wars*, a title stolen from *Raiders of the Lost Ark*, and a plot stolen from the mind of a two-year-old, the film is almost unwatchable.

Interestingly, writer-director Samuel Sherman's next film was the 1987 documentary *Drive-In Madness*, which looks at drive-in movie culture and features an interview with George Romero. I wonder if Romero knew that Sherman had just dealt a blow to the subgenre he so brilliantly created. *Raiders of the Living Dead* writer Brett Piper would not surprisingly go on to pen even worse schlock, including *A Nymphoid Barbarian in Dinosaur Hell* (1990).

Raiders of the Living Dead (1986)

JONATHAN: This Randall is no loony and my grandfather takes him very seriously.

MICHELLE: About what?

JONATHAN: About being attacked by zombies.

MICHELLE: Zombies! You're not making this up?

JONATHAN: Uh uh.

---

28 DAYS LATER (2002)

In the 1990s, zombie video games took over for film as the driver of undead representations in visual media. It wasn't until 2002, with director Danny Boyle's *28 Days Later*, that the subgenre got its next breath of life.

The movie opens as a confused bike messenger wakes from a long coma to find the hospital empty and the streets of London deserted. He is soon chased by raving maniacs that lead him to join forces with a small band of survivors who desperately search for hope and safety in a world gone mad.

Though both Boyle and George Romero rightly agree that the rage-filled humans in *28 Days* aren't technically zombies, the film was wildly successful, and fans across the globe saw it as the next great innovation in the zombie subgenre. Shot on digital video and made for just $8 million, *28 Days Later* grossed an estimated $90 million worldwide and will forever be known as the film that brought us fast zombies.

SHAUN OF THE DEAD (2004)

The 2000s have been boom years for zombie films, such as *Shaun of the Dead* in 2004—a comedy send-up hybrid of Romero's classic *Night of the Living Dead* and O'Bannon's *Return of the Living Dead*—which made fun of zombies a bit but still held on to traditional elements. While Romero was critical of *Return of the Living Dead* in the 1980s, saying that making fun of the monster ruins its potential to horrify, he embraced *Shaun of the Dead* and has since included writer Simon Pegg and director Edgar Wright in cameos in his own zombie movies.

Shaun of the Dead tells the story of two underachieving best friends who are forced to become unlikely heroes when England is overrun by flesh-eating zombies. While *28 Days Later* presents the grim reality of a catastrophic zombie outbreak in gritty super-speed, *Shaun* slows the action down and proves that even though it's the end of the world you can still have a bit of fun.

REC (2007)

Picking up where Danny Boyle's infected left off, Spanish director Paco Plaza gave us what at first appears to be a new and deadly form of rabies in *REC* (2007). As the terrifying story unfolds, we learn that something much more sinister is at work.

The film follows a standard living zombie model, but what makes it unique is that the creatures come into existence as a result of a misguided attempt to cure demonic possession by indentifying the offending substance in a little girl's infected blood. A secret experiment in the penthouse of a Barcelona apartment building goes horribly wrong, unleashing a new virus on the unsuspecting residents. Those infected quickly turn into bloodthirsty maniacs filled with pure rage, while authorities outside seal the building off to prevent the mysterious sickness from spreading.

REC got a shot-for-shot remake in the 2008 American film *Quarantine*, and both have spawned multiple sequels.

ZOMBIELAND (2009)

Considered one of the most profitable zombie movies ever made, *Zombieland* tells the story of four survivors of a catastrophic zombie plague making their way across the American Southwest. It's a wild romp often called America's answer to *Shaun of the Dead*, and its huge success at the box office has been instrumental in the rise of the modern zombie in recent years.

What's most interesting about *Zombieland* isn't the money it raked in but the fact that the flesh-eating creatures it presents aren't dead. While *28 Days Later* introduced a living, fast zombie to the world several years earlier and the *Dawn of the Dead* remake allowed their undead flesh eaters to run in 2004, *Zombieland* is the first movie to ignore the distinction between living and dead zombies. It instead makes a strong argument that it doesn't matter if the raving horde chasing you is alive or not. If they inhabit human bodies, want to eat you, and will stop at nothing to accomplish that goal, they are zombies.

THE CLASSIC ZOMBIE OPEN

An "open" in film-speak is the beginning sequence of a film. Zombie opens reveal that as misunderstood as the modern zombie is in certain living circles, the people who know the absolute least about the undead are the characters in zombie movies themselves. Most of the time, that fact spells disaster for them.

Characters in zombie movies simply don't watch zombie movies. In fact, if you were to ask almost any character at the start of almost any zombie movie of the last fifty years to define a zombie, he or she would have no idea what you were talking about. *A zom-what? Never heard of that.* To be fair, this isn't a convention of zombie movies alone. Characters across all film genres suffer from a com-

plete lack of cinematic reference, as if they'd never seen a single movie in their entire lives.

This may not seem so strange at first, but imagine if your average teen in a contemporary comedy didn't know what Twitter was or had never even heard of the Internet. Imagine an action hero who couldn't warn his girlfriend about the bomb in her trunk because he had no idea what a cell phone was, much less how to use one. Audiences would throw up their hands in disgust.

Plausibility is a key element to the success of any movie. Without it, viewers are jarred from the action and emotion on-screen, and the picture dies a speedy death. That's why filmmakers go to such great lengths to reflect contemporary culture accurately in their work. They make sure the right cars are used, the right slang, the right clothing. Budget allowing, they employ an entire army of professionals devoted to props, sets, and costumes, all with the sole purpose of making the movie look and feel as realistic as possible. But with rare exception, this same standard doesn't hold true when it comes to film references, especially in horror films. And it certainly doesn't hold true in zombie movies.

Zombie movies typically open with the world in an ignorantly blissful state, but soon enough, the dead rise and start eating the living. An obligatory period of confusion and panic sets in, as the public struggles to overcome its utter naïveté about the threat it's facing. The characters have no idea what is coming at them, so they are forced gradually to figure out the rules these new creatures follow. *They don't stay down when you shoot them! Aim for the head! Why is Mom eating the cat?*

Each new movie starts from zero, with no collective knowledge, and then quickly works its way up the information ladder until any remaining survivors are well aware of what it takes to stay alive and are determined to make that happen.

The hit British zombie comedy *Shaun of the Dead* (2004) is the perfect example of this ignorance to zombies. Best friends and epic slackers Ed and Shaun stumble home from a drunken night at the pub to continue the party in their tiny living room. In the wee hours, their responsible roommate, Pete, who went to bed hours earlier, storms in to complain about the loud music and singing. He's got a job. He's got a life. He's not a loser, and he wants to get some sleep!

In the ensuing argument, it's revealed that Pete has a bandage over his right hand. It's a bite. Pete brushes it off as nothing. The discussion moves on, and that's the last we hear of it. Of course, as viewers with at least a smidgen of cultural knowledge about the modern zombie, we know that Pete's bite means he's probably infected, destined to die and be reanimated as a flesh-hungry monster bent on eating Ed and Shaun for breakfast. Sure enough, the next morning, zombie hilarity ensues.

Shaun of the Dead (2004)

ED: What's up with your hand, man?

PETE: I got mugged on the way home from work.

ED: By who?

PETE: I don't know. Some crackheads or something. One of them bit me.

ED: Why did they bite you?

PETE: I don't know! I didn't stop to ask them!

The insertion of this plot device—characters who know nothing of zombies at all living in a film world that has never heard of them—in a savvy comedy like *Shaun of the Dead* shows that it's so commonly used in zombie movies and so absurd that it's a ready-made gag. Another zombie romp, *Zombieland* (2009), uses the same open to the zombie world, but instead of a roommate who is bitten by a crackhead, it's a beautiful neighbor girl who is bitten by a homeless man.

An alternate approach to the classic zombie open is to skip over the obligatory initial confusion by having your hero sleep through the mayhem and wake up only after the world has settled into its new undead state. Other characters can then quickly fill him in on the situation and rules for survival, speeding up the airtime it takes everyone to figure out what these creatures are. I call this the Van Winkle Technique, and it has been used in popular modern zombie franchises such as *28 Days Later* and *The Walking Dead*.

A BUCKET OF BLOOD AND FIVE FRIENDS

In addition to the many actors who got their breaks in the broader horror genre, several big-name directors have launched careers with zombie movies and then gone on to great critical acclaim with more mainstream projects. The success of these early films allowed their careers to move forward and put them in a position to become household names.

Danny Boyle won an Oscar for Best Director for his work on *Slumdog Millionaire* six years after solidifying his spot on the entertainment map with 2002's *28 Days Later*. In 2003, Peter Jackson got his directing Oscar for *The Lord of the Rings:*

The Return of the King, but zombie fans knew him first for his 1992 romp, *Dead Alive*, about a weak-willed son who tries desperately to keep things together after his mother is turned into a raving undead beast. Jackson's second film, 1994's *Heavenly Creatures*, starred Kate Winslet in her first film role and garnered Jackson an Oscar nomination for Best Screenplay.

Zombie movies are perfect launchpads because they're so inexpensive to produce. I always say that anybody with a bucket of fake blood and five friends willing to limp around on camera can make a zombie movie. The British zombie film *Colin*, widely reported to have been made for less than $100, was the surprise hit of the 2009 Cannes Film Festival's film market. It led to writer-director Marc Price landing several other big-budget deals. *Colin* tells a simple zombie story from the title character's point of view as he stumbles home in the midst of a catastrophic outbreak, only to change into a flesh eater himself.

A couple of years earlier, another feature-length zombie film, *Pathogen*, gained national attention not so much for its shoestring budget but because it was made by Emily Hagins, a twelve-year-old girl in Austin, Texas. In *Pathogen*, a group of middle school students must save their town from a mysterious water-borne infection that causes the dead to rise. The film was the subject of a 2009 documentary, *Zombie Girl*.

Some critics carp that the low-budget, anybody-can-make-one approach to zombie movies encourages a lot of schlock to hit the screen, making it even more difficult for the genre to get the respect it deserves. A fair point, but I would argue that the lowered bar also allows talented independent filmmakers to jump into the game without dealing with the prohibitive budgets, outsized egos, and mercurial politics of established studios. Having worked in and around Hollywood for a number of years, I can tell you that this is one hell of a plus.

KNOW YOUR ZOMBIES: HARE KRISHNA

Dawn of the Dead (1978)

Romero's *Dawn of the Dead* created several iconic zombies, but leading the pack is this bald flesh eater in orange robes. The Hare Krishna zombie stalks an indoor shopping mall looking for victims to convert to his new undead religion, much like he did when he was still alive.

Though the Hare Krishna zombie doesn't get a successful kill on-screen, he continues to be popular with merchandisers who've adapted him to everything from action figures to lunch boxes.

ILLUSTRATION BY TERRY CALLEN

31: ZOMBIES ON THE SMALL SCREEN

On February 6, 2011, the NFL's Green Bay Packers and Pittsburgh Steelers faced off in Super Bowl XLV, widely reported to be the most-watched sports event in U.S. television history, with more than 110 million viewers. To capitalize on the massive audience, broadcaster Fox aired a special episode of its hit musical comedy series *Glee* immediately following the game. And what plot device did the creators of *Glee* use to help keep people glued to their seats? Zombies. The rival glee club and football team joined forces and dressed like the undead, culminating in a halftime zombie dance performance that saved the club's season and helped the football team win their game. Zombies saved the day!

Glee, Episode 2.11 (2011)

BRITTANY: Zombie camp was funner than I expected. And the glee club together with the football team is like a double rainbow. A zombie double rainbow.

QUINN: If we go to the cheerleading competition, then we miss the halftime show and we're out of glee club. I'm torn.

SANTANA: I'm not.

BRITTANY: I'm Brittany.

The modern zombie has been a featured guest on a wide range of TV shows, from Comedy Central's long-running animated series *South Park* to NBC's prime-time sitcom *Community*. Even Superman battled a zombielike horde in *Smallville* in 2009. In a one-month period between April and May 2011, the undead appeared or were discussed on Fox's animated comedy *Bob's Burgers*, on ABC's freshman sitcom *Happy Endings*, and on the CBS veteran prime-time hit *The Big Bang Theory*. So completely has the modern zombie infected our TVs that George Romero said he won't be surprised if zombies shamble into *Sesame Street* to hang out with the Count.[67]

Zombies also sell products on TV, from cold medicine to cars. On April 14, 2011, a Ford commercial featured the finalists of *American Idol* season 10 playing zombies more interested in the new Mustang than in eating innocent victims. Not long after Ford's pitch, Honda launched an ad campaign for the 2012 Civic that featured a zombie driving to work, playing golf, and hitting on women at a singles bar.

STAR OF THE SHOW

In 2008 the modern zombie got its first chance to step into a recurring role in the British miniseries *Dead Set,* a fictional account of what happens when the cast of the reality show *Big Brother* is left stranded inside their secure compound while the rest of the world collapses under the weight of a zombie plague. *Dead Set* premiered in the UK in October 2008 to strong ratings and critical acclaim, and was then rebroadcast in January and October 2009. IFC in the United States then picked up the series and aired it for American audiences in October 2010.

In that same month, the AMC original series *The Walking Dead* finally gave zombies a real shot on the small screen in the United States. The story follows small-town police officer Rick Grimes and a collection of fellow survivors in their quest to carve out a life after a global zombie pandemic causes complete societal collapse. In keeping with George Romero's original vision, the action is centered around the personality conflicts within the human ranks, with the zombie threat only serving to increase tension and draw out character flaws. It was an instant hit.

The Walking Dead scored a higher rating in the coveted 18–49 demographic than any drama series in the history of basic cable. Hollywood news outlet *The Wrap* said it was a watershed day for the respected cable network:

> Mad Men *and* Breaking Bad *brought AMC awards, prestige, and the wealthy, well-educated audience that most networks would envy, but* The Walking Dead *has given the network the one thing it didn't have: a flat-out hit.*[68]

The Walking Dead began life as an established graphic novel. It was considered for television adaptation several years before it was finally produced, but it was not the first potential breakthrough zombie series for TV. The 2009 hit zombie movie *Zombieland* was originally developed as a TV series for CBS but was shelved when the studio decided that zombies weren't fit for that medium. Times have changed.

In November 2010, less than one month after *The Walking Dead* premiered, I met with Sharon Levy, executive vice president of original programming for Spike TV. She confirmed that the show's success had turned the entertainment community green with envy, saying that every major television network was in the process of trying to create their own hit zombie show. Though most will never make it out of development hell, here's hoping that more quality zombie programming like *The Walking Dead* is coming to a TV near you soon.

32: ZOMBIE VIDEO GAMES

From the first modern zombie outbreak in a remote Pennsylvania cemetery in 1968's *Night of the Living Dead*, it was just a matter of time before the walking dead reached our own homes. With the rise of zombie console video games in the 1990s, we didn't have to leave the living room anymore to be entertained and terrified by the latest in zombie mayhem. What's more, video games throw the audience into the undead action in a way that films can't.

Kicking off the craze, video game maker Capcom released *Resident Evil* for the Sony PlayStation system in 1996, changing the face of horror gaming forever and becoming one of the biggest franchises of all time. With more than fifteen games, spinoff comics, novels, and action figures, *Resident Evil* was instrumental in the revitalization of zombies in film, too.

The *Resident Evil* story takes place in the fictional Raccoon City. We follow a team of SWAT officers as they investigate reports of mass cannibalism and the disappearance of some of their colleagues. With limited supplies and a complex mystery to unravel, players are taken through an undead maze of creaking doors and shambling corpses that lurch forward from all sides. Though *Resident Evil* wasn't the first zombie video game—that title goes to the relatively forgettable *Zombie Zombie* (1984)—at the time of its release, it was unquestionably the most inventive and compelling zombie game ever made.

Senior editor of *GamePro* magazine Patrick Shaw says that *Resident Evil* brought zombie video games to prominence, and its influence on the industry as a whole is profound:

> *The series is essentially responsible for legitimizing the horror genre in games. The scarcity of ammunition and supplies like first-aid kits, which you'll see in most horror-themed games today, is directly borrowed from* Resident Evil.

George Romero says that *Resident Evil* and the zombie games that followed it have driven the popularity of zombies in recent years much more than films.[69] Paco Plaza, director of the innovative Spanish living-zombie franchise *REC*, has explained that *Resident Evil* influenced his zombie filmmaking techniques. His unique approach of abruptly shifting the audience's camera view came from playing zombie video games for hours on end.[70]

BEYOND RACCOON CITY

Electronic zombie games are such an economic and entertainment force that many game franchises that are not inherently zombie-related have shoehorned the undead into their projects, either as add-ons or as completely new spinoffs of their original concepts. *Red Dead Redemption* is a popular Wild West video game released by Rockstar Games in May 2010, as a follow-up to their successful 2004 offering *Red Dead Revolver.* Five months after it hit stores, Rockstar introduced a zombie plague sweeping across the *Redemption* frontier with its downloadable add-on called *Undead Nightmare*. The western-meets-zombie concept was such a hit that in November, *Red Dead Redemption: Undead Nightmare* was offered as a stand-alone game.

That same month the first-person military shooter *Call of Duty: Black Ops* was released with its own zombie spin. Developed by Treyarch, it is the seventh installment of the wildly popular *Call of Duty* franchise. Within twenty-four hours of hitting store shelves, *Black Ops* sold more than 7 million copies worldwide, and it went on to top $1 billion in sales in less than two months, due in no small part to its zombie mode, which features John F. Kennedy, Richard Nixon, and Fidel Castro fighting the undead inside the Pentagon.

An additional downloadable map pack, *Black Ops: Escalation*, was released in May 2011 featuring expanded zombie game play titled *Call of the Dead*. Set in an isolated region of the old Soviet Union, *Escalation*'s zombie mode includes new characters, impressive cinematic action, and even George Romero as a zombie. The game's director, Dave Anthony, adds:

> This is Treyarch's tribute to the legendary George Romero, who truly defined the zombie genre and whose incredible work has been such an inspiration to our team.[71]

Despite many exciting innovations, zombie video games continue to follow a common framework that shapes nearly all zombie stories, whether they're on the big screen, on desktop screens, or on little handheld ones.

Bernard Perron is professor of cinema at the Université de Montréal and editor of *Horror Video Games: Essays on the Fusion of Fear and Play*. When it comes to the scholarly review of zombie games, there isn't anybody on the planet better qualified. He observes:

Why would zombie video games differ from the canoni-cal post-Romero zombie plot? Bottom line, interactive or not, one has to survive the zombie apocalypse. But even though most games are just variations on the same theme, it doesn't mean that the genre isn't evolving in new and in-teresting ways.

It seems the evolution in electronic zombie gaming has actu-ally mirrored the evolution of zombie films. George Romero's *Night of the Living Dead*, which established the subgenre, was made with a tiny budget, so it had to take place in an isolated area—a farmhouse—where fewer than a couple of dozen attackers could represent a national zombie outbreak. Simi-larly, the groundbreaking *Resident Evil* set its action in con-fined spaces where just a few electronic zombies could do the same.

A decade later, Romero's second film was made with a bigger budget and set in a shopping mall, using hundreds of zombie extras to create the mass hordes, rather than im-plying them with a limited cast. Similarly, Capcom's popular zombie video game franchise *Dead Rising* (2006) innovates on *Resident Evil* ten years after its release by introducing massive zombie hordes on-screen, also in a shopping mall. And just as running zombies upped the ante in films and became the new zombie norm with the *Dawn of the Dead* remake of 2004, the *Left 4 Dead* franchise introduced fast ghouls to gaming in 2008. But the newest evolution of the zombie game isn't found on the console or the computer but at the app store.

With the explosion of high-tech products in recent years, such as Apple's iPhone and iPad, programmers across the planet have introduced hundreds of thousands of download-able applications. From making electronic fart noises to checking the calorie count of a bacon cheeseburger, Apple's trademarked slogan seems to hold true: "There's an app for that." And in the first few months of 2010, no pop-culture app sold better than *Plants vs. Zombies.*

This lighthearted tower defense game moved 300,000 copies worth more than $1 million in just nine days, ranking it number one in both units sold and gross revenue on Apple's charts within twenty-four hours of its launch on February 15, 2010.

Much the way online video has allowed new filmmakers to gain exposure for their work, leading to innovations in that medium, mobile gaming is ushering in a new way of playing in the zombie world.

Read Dead Revolver—Undead Nightmare (2010)

JOHN: Come out. It's okay. Come out, I don't bite. Bad joke. I mean, come out.

GIRL: They got my family, mister.

JOHN: And mine, I fear.

GIRL: I saw my momma rip my daddy's face off!

WORST GAMES EVER

There's no shortage of bad zombie movies, and there's no shortage of disappointing zombie games to go around. Many critics argue that the most disappointing zombie game title ever released is *Land of the Dead: Road to Fiddler's Green*, loosely based on George Romero's 2005 film. Gamespot's Alex Navarro suggests that it falls just short of approaching brilliance in its sheer awfulness:

The game shuffles along at a sluggish, depressing pace while pieces of it literally fall apart at the seams. This is either one of the most avant-garde pieces of gaming artistry to ever find its way to the retail market, or the absolute worst game ever.[72]

For my money, though, the worst zombie game on the planet is *Attack of the Sunday School Zombies* from Sunday Software. In this illogical mess, players take on the role of Super Kenz the Bible Kid, spouting passages from scripture and firing a crossbow loaded with chocolate doughnuts at zombies of all ages as they complain about being bored in church. If Kenz's aim is true, she subdues the zombies with doughnuts long enough to teach them why their bad attitudes are "lame" and how to be better churchgoers.

WHAT'S NEXT?

Despite several noted innovations in zombie video games over the past fifteen years, they still closely follow a common framework borrowed from zombie movies. None of them have taken advantage of the immersive quality of gaming to construct a world that presents realistic zombie survival scenarios and challenges. That may soon change.

Formed in 2009, Undead Labs is a video game development company in Seattle, Washington, with the singular focus of creating the first-ever true zombie survival console game. Founder Jeff Strain says that the project is a logical next step in the evolution of zombie gaming:

When fans leave the theater after a great zombie movie they're all talking about what they would have done in that situation. Zombie survival is a key element to the popularity of the living dead today, but video games haven't kept up with this reality.

Undead Labs' plan as of 2011 is to produce a highly polished console zombie game for Xbox, followed by a massively multiplayer online world. Hopefully, they'll succeed.

33: ZOMBIE LITERATURE

The doorbell rings. You glance outside and spot a group of carolers dressed as if they'd walked off the pages of a Charles Dickens novel. Christmas carolers? It's the right time of year, the end of December, so when they start humming a traditional song, you open the door. Oops. Too late. The nice singers on the porch aren't a local church group. They're actually the walking dead. They're all dressed like rotting zombies, and though the tune they sing harks back to the carols of a bygone era, the lyrics are rotten and twisted:

> Fresh brains roasting on an open fire,
> Zombies chewing off your nose.

In 2009, author Michael Spradlin released his book of zombie Christmas carols, *It's Beginning to Look a Lot Like Zombies.* Now carolers around the country can join the celluloid undead and the electronic undead in your home.

If movies are the old guard in zombie culture and video games are the established player, then zombie literature is the new kid on the block and making quite an impact. As of the end of January 2010, there were no fewer than five zombie-themed books on the *New York Times* bestseller list. At the end of January 2011, there were nine books on the list, with many others rising and falling off over that twelve-month period. Zombie lit has hit the big time, and it seems that from Jane Austen's *Pride and Prejudice* to Studs Terkel's oral history of World War II, nothing is safe from loose or direct adaptation for the ravenous zombie market.

Like video games, books are giving back to the medium that created the modern zombie, with dozens of novels being optioned for Hollywood adaptation in recent years. This multiplatform success has helped push zombies from a fringe subculture to the mainstream, and the evidence of their arrival is clear in the names of the players. Brad Pitt's production company optioned Max Brooks's zombie novel *World War Z*, slating it for a large-budget studio production. When the undead are mentioned in the same breath as A-list celebrities, you know they've hit the big time.

But why did it take more than three decades for the undead to make a real impact in publishing? Kim Paffenroth is professor of religious studies at Iona College and an author of several fiction and nonfiction zombie books. He argues that the appeal of zombies has traditionally been a visual phenomenon:

> *Zombies are cool to look at, either when they're having pieces of themselves blown off with gunfire, or when they're tearing a screaming person limb from limb. That makes them seem much better suited to film, video games, and comic books.*

The challenge for writers has been to find a way to make an inherently visual creature engaging on the page. Often, this means roping in familiar characters, such as Jane Austen's Mr. Darcy, or focusing on the character development of the survivors. From accounts of the strained relationships of the living to detailing zombie combat, strategy, and tactics, authors have attacked the subgenre from all angles in the past decade.

THE BROOKS FACTOR

In nonfiction, Max Brooks launched the zombie instructional manual craze with his groundbreaking *Zombie Survival Guide*, published in 2003. At the time, the book was cutting-edge and such a hit that it convinced publishers to snap up guides that claimed to teach everything from proper zombie etiquette to the official military policy for dealing with an undead outbreak.

Brooks followed up that effort with his 2006 novel *World War Z*, making him the biggest name in the world of zombie publishing and putting zombie fiction squarely on the mainstream map. The book was originally called *The Zombie Wars*, but his publishers didn't want the word *zombie* in the title because they thought it wouldn't appeal to a broad audience. So he shortened *Zombie* to *Z* for the more global-sounding *World War Z*. Now, less than five years later, anything with the word *zombie* in the title is hot in the publishing world, as we'll see below.

Both of Brooks's books are regulars on the *New York Times* bestseller lists in their categories, but when he shopped *The Zombie Survival Guide* in the late 1990s, no publishing house would touch it. It took upward of five years from the time Brooks wrote the book for it to reach store shelves, and even then, only a few thousand copies were produced in the first printing. This wasn't initially a moneymaking scheme, as it has become for some writers since. Brooks did it because he loved zombies, and he's looking forward to getting his hands on the next great zombie book to come along:

I hope that someone out there right now is writing an amazing zombie book, looking at the monster from a completely new angle. I love reading great zombie stories and can't wait to be knocked out of my chair.

MASHUP MAYHEM

In March 2009, *Pride and Prejudice and Zombies* by Jane Austen and Seth Grahame-Smith hit stores with a bang. Billed as a classic romance with ultraviolent zombie mayhem, the novel is 85 percent original text from Austen and 15 percent Grahame-Smith's undead action. The mix proved to be pure sales gold for publisher Quirk Books. The comedic mashup quickly climbed the *New York Times* best-seller list, spawning two sequels and a Hollywood film deal.

Pride and Prejudice and Zombies follows Elizabeth Bennet and her sisters as they defend their quiet English village  from roaming undead hordes decades after the country is overrun by zombies. Trying to cash in on the newly discovered zombie mashup market, dozens of other classic stories and characters soon received an undead makeover, including *The Wizard of Oz, The Adventures of Huckleberry Finn*, Santa Claus, and the Beatles. Horror genre critic Juvanka Vuckavic dismisses zombie mashups as one-trick ponies and expects the fad to quickly fizzle out, but there still seems no end in sight.

For my money, one of the better mashups of the past several years is another Quirk Books release, the 2010 zombie romp *Night of the Living Trekkies.* Set at a science-fiction convention, a strange virus soon transforms Klingons, Vulcans, and Ferengi into flesh-eating zombies. Even the nonsensical inclusion of Princess Leia from *Star Wars* doesn't slow down the fun.

Before Quirk wrote the rules for classic literature zombie mashups, iconic comic book publisher Marvel was paving the way with their legion of undead superheroes in their five-issue series *Marvel Zombies*. With a first book released in late 2005, *Marvel Zombies* features an alien virus that turns heroes like Iron Man, Spider-Man, the Hulk, and Wolverine into raving beasts with all the bite wounds and rotting flesh of any traditional flesh eater. Some argue that the resulting super-creatures aren't actually zombies because they are sometimes intelligent, sometimes invincible, and sometimes can even be cured, highlighting the inherent conflict in taking a uniquely scientific infection like zombieism and applying it to the decidedly supernatural world of Marvel.

My favorite comic mashup comes from IDW Publishing. Building on their popular comic series *Zombies vs. Robots*, IDW turned to name-brand Hollywood properties like *Star Trek*, *Transformers*, *G.I. Joe*, and *Ghostbusters* in order to produce crossover comics in which these beloved characters battle zombies under the series name *Infestation*. The first one was released in January 2011. I'm waiting for them to go whole-hog with *Zombies vs. Malibu Barbie*, *Zombies vs. NHL All-Stars*, or even *Zombies vs. The Brady Bunch*.

RIDING THE GRAVY TRAIN

From famine to feast: Where there was virtually no zombie literature in the thirty-five years after George Romero first created his flesh eaters in *Night of the Living Dead*, now readers and publishers are eating it up. Some say that's not such a good thing.

In countless discussions with other zombie enthusiasts and experts, I've always argued that the explosion of zombie literature in recent years can only be a good thing. Just as there are good, bad, and ugly zombie movies, why shouldn't there also be the same quality variety in books? I like them all and read them all. But an article published in the October 2010 issue of *The Writer* magazine caused me to reverse my view.

The Writer is a monthly publication with a stated mission to provide advice and inspiration for today's writer. The article in question, "Dawn of the Undead," is a detailed outline for capitalizing on the current publishing frenzy around zombies even if you don't have any personal interest in them. Never seen a zombie movie? No problem. Don't know who George Romero is? Big deal. What really hit a nerve for me was that the article went so far as to say that you "don't even have to like zombies to get a career boost from them." That seems too shallow and predatory even for zombies.

Scooby-Doo on Zombie Island (1998)

FRED: There's nothing here now. Are you sure you saw a zombie?

SHAGGY: Like, we know a zombie when we see one.

SCOOBY: Reah! Rombie!

But like it or not, the *Writer* article reflects publishing reality. Even if you don't want to write about zombies at all, just put the word *zombie* in the title of your book, and you can sell more copies. *I Talked with a Zombie* is a collection of interviews with horror-movie insiders. None of the interviewees, however, has worked on a modern zombie movie. The word *zombie* doesn't even appear inside the pages of the book, but the publishers slapped *zombie* in the title and cashed in.

Here's another example: the *Mammoth Book of Zombie Comics*. More than sixty pages are devoted to a story about a mummy. Another story centers on a haunted painting. I suppose calling it the *Mammoth Book of Monster Comics* wouldn't have gotten as much attention. So they camouflaged the mummies and haunted paintings in their marketing by plastering traditional modern zombie hordes on the cover in order to drive sales. In truth, I liked the book, and most of its stories focus on zombies. But what if a book of vampire comics had mummies in it? What if a book of aliens had a story about werewolves? Would that fly?

Don't get me wrong. I love pretty much any zombie book I can get my hands on, no matter what the intention of the author was when writing it. I want to read anything and everything. But now that money is in the driver's seat, there is a clear risk of losing sight of the love of the subgenre that led to so many impressive and inventive works in the first place.

34: THE DEAD WALK

On Saturday, April 2, 2011, hundreds of people dressed as zombies and took to the streets of Madison, Wisconsin, to protest Governor Scott Walker's controversial move to eliminate the collective-bargaining rights of most state workers. Shuffling along, they voiced their frustration with what they saw as the stupidity of the state's leadership by moaning a traditional zombie chant: "What do we want? BRAINS! When do we want them? BRAINS!"

One marching zombie said that he applied gray face paint and rubber peeling skin to make a statement that collective bargaining should be a fundamental labor right in the United States, noting that the fact that the protesters were all zombies worked to keep things civil:

> This keeps the pressure on Walker while getting everybody smiling at the same time. It puts lightheartedness into a very serious situation.[73]

Sadly, the governor declined my request for comment about how it felt to be threatened by a zombie mob.

But why did the protesters choose to look like zombies rather than some other kind of monster? Many other creatures provide fabulous metaphors for the failures of political leadership. Why not vampires because government action is sucking the life out of its citizens? Why not sharks because government is circling around its innocent employees? Why not werewolves because in Wisconsin it's still chilly in early April, and the costume fur would be nice insulation? More importantly, why do hundreds of thousands of people across the globe dress up like zombies each year and march from one place to another for no reason other than to march from one place to another dressed like zombies?

Brendan Riley is a professor of new media and cultural studies at Columbia College in Chicago, where he teaches a class on zombies in popular media. His theory is that walking like a zombie with other zombies taps into a deep-seated desire to break social boundaries and occasionally act improperly. Plus, it's just a really good time. As he puts it:

> Zombie walks are really fun. They provide an excuse to get together with other zombie fans, to dress up and show off, but without the pressure of being a solitary performer.

Whatever the reason for their popularity, there is no question that zombie walks are an essential element in the cultural explosion of the modern zombie.

So where did it all start?

THE FIRST ZOMBIE WALK

Thea Munster, a recent film-school graduate, wanted to do something a little different, so she asked her friends if they had any interest in painting their faces like corpses, throwing on some old rags, and walking through their suburban Toronto neighborhood with her. Unfortunately, they flatly rejected the idea as stupid. Who would want to do something like that? What would be the point?

Munster didn't really have a good answer for them, but she also couldn't let the idea die. So she hung up posters around town for anyone who might want to join her on her morbid stroll. The next week, on a gray and rainy October day in 2003, seven strangers dressed like zombies met at Necropolis Cemetery near the University of Toronto campus and walked together.

Passing neighbors didn't know what to make of the spectacle. As Munster explains, a young couple driving by screeched to a halt in the middle of the road in complete shock:

Another person came out of her house, saw us, and then turned around and scooted back inside. A man walking up the block ahead saw us and actually started running away. It was hard not to laugh. I guess no one had ever seen anything like it at the time.

Before Munster's initiative, marketing firms had paraded zombie extras to publicize films and other events, but this was the first time anyone walked just for the sake of walking. They didn't do it for profit or publicity or even charity. They just walked.

The following year, the undead gang of walkers in Toronto grew larger, and by year three, with more than a hundred expected participants, cemetery officials informed Munster that they had instituted a "no costume" policy and she would have to move elsewhere. She took the event to a more central location in Toronto, and the rest is history.

What started as a handful of oddballs grew into thousands of oddballs walking through the center of Toronto. At one point, the police tried to shut them down, calling the walk a drain on resources. They even had a scare near a bus stop until an investigation into a mysterious pool of blood showed that it was corn syrup used by one of the marchers.

Eventually, the Toronto officials endorsed the walk as a benefit to the city. If you can't beat them, join them—another enduring motto of the modern zombie. And now organized zombie walks can be found all across the world.

THE GROWING PLAGUE

Since Guinness World Records first certified Pittsburgh, Pennsylvania's zombie walk as the largest to date in 2006, many cities have aimed their sights on claiming that prize. From Toronto, Canada, to Brisbane, Australia, official and unofficial records are set and broken multiple times each year. Nottingham, England, earned the distinction in 2008. The following year the title changed hands three times before Herefordshire, England, took the top spot with a zombie horde over four thousand strong. Seattle, Washington, briefly claimed supremacy in 2010 before Asbury Park, New Jersey, was named the winner by Guinness after they completed their official tabulations in early April 2011. Dozens of cities are planning to make their run for the crown, ensuring that zombie walks will continue to grow in size and number for the foreseeable future.

Zombie (1979)

PAOLA: They've found another one, haven't they? Tell the truth!

DAVID: Now calm down.

PAOLA: Where did they find it?

DAVID: You really mustn't drink so much, darling.

Innovating on the standard walk model, zombie flash mobs have sprung up in recent years across the world, too. A zombie flash mob is an unannounced assemblage of people dressed as the undead that shamble about a public place like a mall or main city street. Regular flash mobs as a rule typically feature normally dressed pedestrians who suddenly begin performing a choreographed dance or some other creative action in unison to the delight of surprised onlookers, the classic example being the videotaped flash mob in New York City's Grand Central Terminal.

Zombie flash mobs don't dance. They don't pose together as an elaborate living art piece. They don't do anything except be zombies, so they more closely mimic the experience of a real zombie outbreak with their uncoordinated movements and genuine spontaneity. They also don't apply for permits or notify the proper authorities in advance, making their infestation seem sudden and organic.

Better even than zombie flash mobs, zombie pub crawls are another variation on the traditional walk that involves shambling from one bar to the next, drinking ever more along the way. The notion of being among a bunch of people dressed as zombies doesn't sound fun to me—it sounds alarming—but if I were forced to do a zombie walk of some kind, a pub crawl would be my first choice. Though it makes no sense from a survival standpoint, the end of the world is a lot more palatable with a cold beer in hand.

35: FUN WITH ZOMBIES

With the surge in popularity of the modern zombie in recent years, all manner of undead events may be happening near you. There's San Francisco's zombie drag queen roller derby, which features queens racing to the finish line while zombie queens try to eat them. There are zombie charity evenings, like the one in St. Louis that raised funds for Direct Relief International to benefit the victims of Japan's 2011 earthquake, and zombie canned food drives, like the one held in conjunction with San Diego's World Zombie Day in 2008. There's the new zombie beach party in Asbury Park, New Jersey, which promises to be an annual event featuring a zombie kissing booth, dunk the zombie, and brain volleyball. You can even attend zombie plays. In the summer of 2011 the Bushwick Star in Brooklyn, New York, premiered *Death Valley: A Western Horror Play*. The cast included western stock character favorites—a con man, a whore, a doctor, and an Apache—who together face the biggest challenge that could befall anyone west of the Mississippi—a zombie infestation.

When it comes to zombie fun, nothing seems outside the bounds of the possible and popular. Just as actual zombies could appear at any time, zombie events are year-round opportunities for donning pancake makeup, fake blood, and your favorite shredded outfit to lurch around with friends and friendly strangers. But there's no better month to express your interest in the living dead than May, because May is Zombie Awareness Month.

ZOMBIE AWARENESS MONTH

Why is May Zombie Awareness Month instead of October? Because Halloween actually has nothing to do with zombies.

Celebrated annually at the end of October, Halloween seems primarily an excuse for kids to carve pumpkins, dress up in goofy costumes, and demand free candy from their neighbors. But this witching holiday, originally called All-Hallows' Eve, meaning the evening before All Hallows' Day, or All Saints Day, long held religious significance evolving from a blend of European pagan and folk traditions deeply rooted in myth and superstition.

Nicholas Rogers is a professor of history at York University and author of *Halloween: From Pagan Ritual to Party Night.*

He explains that the holiday originally reflected fears about supernatural threats, and these motifs are still with us today. Rogers discusses dozens of traditional Halloween monsters in his work, but zombies are not mentioned once.

Witches, ghosts, and vampires, all staples of the season, are otherworldly creatures of old, filled with mysticism, unusual powers, or spiritual significance. The modern zombie, on the other hand, is a biologically based entity that reflects thoroughly modern fears. Grounded in empirical science and reflecting contemporary urban society, the modern zombie has nothing to do with Old World legends.

More importantly, the film that single-handedly created the modern zombie in 1968, George Romero's *Night of the Living Dead*, is set in the month of May. What more fitting month could there be?

Since 2007, concerned citizens and zombie enthusiasts have donned gray ribbons in honor of Zombie Awareness Month and participated in a wide range of awareness-raising activities such as zombie walks, zombie theme parties, and zombie charity drives. The gray ribbon is meant to signify the undead menace that threatens our modern light of day, and the organized events are meant for fun. From May 1 through 31, people across the globe take this small step to acknowledge the coming danger that we may all soon face.

But you don't have to wait until May to get involved in zombie mayhem, as events are taking place every day in countries around the world.

HUMANS VS. ZOMBIES

In 2005, Chris Weed and Brad Sappington of Goucher College started a modified game of tag they called Humans vs. Zombies (HvZ). With just thirty-two people playing the first fall, the game grew quickly and then spread virally across the Internet as dozens of Goucher students posted photos and videos online. Today, HvZ is played at hundreds of colleges and universities across the country, as well as at high schools, military bases, summer camps, and even public libraries.

Goucher is the only college in America that requires study abroad as a graduation requirement. As a result, Goucher students have spread the word of Humans vs. Zombies all over the world, and the game is now played in countries such as Brazil, Denmark, Australia, England, and Canada. In fact, HvZ is active on every continent except Antarctica, although a team of South Pole researchers have expressed interest in setting up a game at their outpost.

In Humans vs. Zombies, a group of human players attempts to survive a "zombie outbreak" by outsmarting a growing number of zombie players. But the rules are fluid, and the game's creators encourage each independent player group to modify them as they see fit.

Joe Sklover was among the first to play HvZ at Goucher, and he now manages the game, helping new schools set up their own versions:

> We provide rules but want people to adapt them to the environment. For example, in some games, zombies don't starve to death, while in others, they have to kill a certain number of humans per day to keep playing.

He went on to say that even though it's a game, Humans vs. Zombies can drive people to act just as desperately as they might in a real undead outbreak. Sklover himself once feared he would have to quit the game because he was going out of town and the rules state that you need to be on campus at least once a day. There were only a handful of players remaining, so Sklover set a trap for his human counterparts and fed them to the zombie horde. All's fair in love, war, and zombies.

The game has been profiled by the Associated Press, the *Washington Post*, the *Boston Globe*, *ESPN The Magazine*, and a whole lot of college papers. Stephen Colbert even named Humans vs. Zombies the number one threat to America in 2008.

ZOMBIE LARP

Imagine being trapped in a sealed building packed with zombies. You have a few weapons and supplies, but in the end, you know the raving horde will overwhelm your defenses and you'll be killed. OK, now imagine doing it for fun. Welcome to Zombie LARP, or live-action role-playing games.

In an abandoned underground NATO bunker in the heart of Germany, zombie enthusiasts come together to play out just that scenario. Five stories underground and in almost complete darkness, they try to survive using only their modified Nerf rifles and their wits. A head shot kills the attacking zombies that approach from all sides. Anything less, and you're toast.

IT specialist Manuel Kuss believes that the undead are relevant across the cultural landscape because they feel inherently real. That's why they work so well in movies and video games, and the same holds true in LARP:

In a recent game, a group of players barricaded themselves in a house, and a horde of zombies spent an entire night trying to fight their way in. After two or three hours, one of the survivors inside got so scared she had a panic attack.

Kuss has been participating in LARP for more than a decade, but he says that zombie-themed games are a phenomenon of just the past few years. Until now, live fantasy role playing has been the stuff of *Star Trek* aficionados or Renaissance Fair enthusiasts. The documentary *Darkon*, for example, follows a long-running medieval fantasy gaming club in Baltimore. The film won the Audience Award at the 2006 South by Southwest Film Festival. That was three years before the first zombie LARP was played in Germany. Who knows? Perhaps three years from now, zombies will be LARPing in your neighbor-hood.

ZOMBIE CONVENTIONS

Zombies have infected all manner of pop-culture conventions for years, from San Diego's massive international comic-book and geek-culture convention Comic-Con to regional horror and science-fiction gatherings around the world. Often conventions that have nothing directly to do with zombies include the living dead in their programs to drive traffic and spark interest. In 2011, Combat Con, a Las Vegas gathering of medieval fantasy role-playing and western martial arts enthusiasts, featured panels on zombie defense and preparedness. Zombie Klingons have even been spotted shambling through the halls of *Star Trek* conventions.

My favorite infusion of zombies into general pop culture is the Zombie Apocafest. For several years BrickCon, the annual Lego enthusiasts' convention, included an extensive zombie apocalypse display created entirely from little interlocking bricks and plastic doo-dads. Dubbed the Zombie Apocafest, this mini-cityscape overrun by Lego zombies was built by a horde of dedicated artists. Awards were handed out for best zombie survival vehicle and best zombiefied building.

Though horror conventions across the planet invariably include zombies as a main feature, it wasn't until 2010 that the first dedicated zombie-culture convention was launched. The annual ZomBcon took place in Seattle in late October and featured some of the biggest names in zombie culture, including George Romero and Max Brooks.

The three-day program offered presentations, workshops,

and unique fan events such as the Prom of the Living Dead, an Evil Dead Wedding, and professional scientists and strategists discussing the real-life possibilities of survival. As ZomBcon producer Ryan Reiter observed:

> Zombie walks and games like Humans vs. Zombies are present in almost every city around the world. Zombie video games and movies generate huge interest. It was only right that zombies should finally get their own convention and stop having to piggyback on somebody else's gig.

ZomBcon returned to Seattle in 2011 with plans to move to different cities and countries in the future.

While the convention did feature non-zombie activities in its first two years, such as screenings of the movies *Fight Club* and *A Clockwork Orange*, as well as special guests from the vampire series *True Blood*, it is the first major convention to commit to giving the starring role in its event to the modern zombie.

ZOMBIE PROM

Along with zombie walks, zombie proms are current cultural favorites. They're very similar to the actual prom you remember from high school, but instead of living students in dated prom outfits, they're attended by zombies in dated prom outfits. It's cathartic and occasionally beneficial for charities.

In a dual rejection of the conventional romantic requirements of proms and Valentine's Day traditions, the band Saint Motel's third annual Zombie Prom was held in Los Angeles on Valentine's weekend in 2011 at the historic Alexandria Hotel. As with most zombie proms, the evening included a costume contest and the crowning of the Zombie Prom king and queen. A portion of proceeds from the event was donated to the Brain Research Institute at UCLA. The next weekend the Que Sera club in Long Beach, California, hosted their third annual Sweetheart Massacre Prom featuring zombie bands and a zombie burlesque show starring Miss Fever Blister. Although some zombie proms get more press than others, you can find them across North America. The zombie prom craze was even adapted to the big screen in the 2008 film *Dance of the Dead*, in which the nerds, geeks, and outcasts of a high school save their more popular classmates on prom night by battling invading zombies with garden tools and guitars.

ZOMBIE MUSIC

The first all-zombie band to make a splash in the United States was Nashville's Zombie Bazooka Patrol when the video for their song "Zombie Shake" aired nationally on *The Early Show* in 2007. They also appeared that year in full zombie face paint on Fox's short-lived reality show *The Next Great American Band*. It was a promising start, but the show crashed and burned, as did the band soon thereafter.

Hailing from Madison, Wisconsin, the Zombeatles have made a name for themselves over the past several years by performing garage-rock parodies of classic Beatles tunes with new zombiefied lyrics. Musician and horror director Rob Zombie chose the group's video for their song "A Hard Day's Night of the Living Dead" as one of his top YouTube picks of 2007, and in 2009 the band released their album *Meat the Zombeatles* and companion mockumentary *All You Need Is Brains.* The Zombeatles continue to tour across the U.S.

On the left coast, Zombie Surf Camp in San Diego plays

surf horror punk with their own spin on zombie music and lyrics. With some songs that can be interpreted either plain human or with a zombie bent, such as "What's Eating You?," the costumed undead quintet has played everywhere from a local Rotary Club to a Hells Angels rally. When asked if the band's recent success is due to an uptick in general zombie popularity, member Moon Zoggy says he can't be sure:

> When we play, we put out a lot of energy. I'd like to think that people are responding to that rather than our rotting corpses, but realistically, I have to assume that it's a factor that mostly seems to work in our favor.

And finally, Dead Man's Bones is an indie rock band led by acclaimed film actor Ryan Gosling. The band has collaborated extensively with the Los Angeles–based Silverlake Conservatory of Music Children's Choir, started by musician Flea of Red Hot Chili Peppers fame. Although not strictly a zombie band, Dead Man's Bones does explore macabre themes in their music, and their song "My Body's a Zombie for You" was the winner of the 2009 Zombie Research Society Award for excellence in zombie culture.

ZOMBIE STRIPPERS

Zombie Strippers is a 2008 trashy, straight-to-video movie starring porn star Jenna Jameson as, you guessed it, a stripper who turns into a zombie and eats all of the patrons at her club. She even inexplicably does a naked dance routine as an undead flesh eater. So if you're into that sort of thing, you might want to check it out. The movie received a bit of attention when it was released for no other reason than it starred a naked Jenna Jameson.

What you may not know is that there are actual zombie strippers dancing at actual clubs across the United States and in other countries. Classed up a bit, they are normally called zombie burlesque shows. A perfect example is the Bada Bing Babes of Jacksonville, Florida. On March 28, 2011, this burlesque troupe painted their scantily clad bodies like zombies and danced the night away. The audience even got in on the action with the help of a professional makeup artist who zombiefied anyone who walked through the door.

For those who like their zombies a little more hard-core, the 2006 film *Porn of the Dead* features zombie-on-zombie sex. I don't understand the appeal, but apparently some find it more titillating to watch zombies than humans. Fans of the film hope its "artistic merits" shine through, but I don't think they're talking about the creative makeup job or the dialogue.

ZOMBIE SPORTS

In 2009, the Zombie Research Society posted a pie chart that breaks down the difference between human sporting interests and zombie sporting interests. In zombie survival terms I'm not sure how helpful it will be, but it does illustrate an important fact: zombies have almost no hobbies other than eating you. While humans enjoy baseball, basketball, badminton, car racing, pole vaulting, and so forth, zombies apparently enjoy only three sports: competitive eating, shotgun dodging, and a bit of golf. The golf is a stretch if you ask me, but you get the point.

But it turns out that if you're human and dressed up as a zombie, playing sports can be fun. The catch is that you also have to move like a zombie, which makes some sports less viable than others. Alternatively, you could stay human and practice interacting with zombies in a sporting atmosphere. The two most prominent zombie sports so far, zombie kickball and zombie shooting, demonstrate either option.

Human kickball is a game consisting of two teams, three bases, one home plate, and a big red ball. Played like baseball, the object is to score more runs than the opposing team. Zombie kickball is similar to human kickball except that the undead participants shamble from base to base in no particular hurry. The outfielders shamble too. The game kicked off in Portland, Maine, in 2006 with an annual charity match between opposing zombie teams. It's a loosely organized but well-attended community event with enthusiastic players representing all walks of life, including local politicians, pillars of the community, artists, and social misfits, along with zombie fanatics and athletes just looking for a cool kickball game.

Zombie shoots involve live human players shooting life-size zombie replica targets as a kind of fun-meets-pandemic-self-defense-practice. In October 2008, the Langhorne Rod and Gun Club in Bucks County, Pennsylvania, hosted a moving zombie shoot featuring mobile targets on pulleys stationed around a walking course. The event was so packed and got such word of mouth in gun circles that they had to limit the 2009 entries and handle accommodations for out-of-towners traveling from afar. In July 2011, firearms manufacturer DPMS Panther Arms in St. Cloud, Minnesota, hosted their fourth annual Outbreak Omega, an all-day zombie shoot featuring several hundred competitors vying for prizes. The event has grown every year and seems poised to become one of the country's premier zombie shoots.

ZOMBIE PRODUCTS

There is no end to the zombie products available these days. I've seen zombie-repellent spray, zombie-proof underwear, zombie energy drinks, zombie beef jerky, zombie eyeball candy, zombie necklaces, zombie garden gnomes, zombie artwork, zombie weapons of all sizes and shapes, and even Russian zombie nesting dolls. But vegan zombie brain cupcake soap wins the award for the strangest product I've encountered in recent years. Why are there gooey green brains in a cupcake? Why are they cola scented? I have no idea, but like everything else zombie related, it works!

So surf the Web, visit your local zombie products retailer, join fellow enthusiasts, and enjoy all things zombie as long as you can, because when the real zombies arrive you won't have time anymore to practice your zombie kickball, attend those zombie conventions, or rearrange your zombie garden gnomes in the front yard.

KNOW YOUR ZOMBIES: ED
Shaun of the Dead (2003)

Though Shaun's best friend, Ed, turns into a zombie, he happily lives in the toolshed out back and still likes to play video games. In fact, released from the pressures of having to keep a job and pay rent, Ed gets to leave all the stress and social logistics to Shaun. Sometimes things don't change, despite the zombie apocalypse.

Shaun of the Dead gives us a world in which your friends can still be your friends, even if they're zombies. Somehow I doubt we will be so lucky.

ILLUSTRATION BY JEFF McMILLAN

36: ZOMBIE ORGANIZATIONS

When looking at the explosion of communal, free-for-all zombie activity across the planet, I'm reminded of the late Groucho Marx's joke about the exclusive club culture of America: "I refuse to join any club that would have me as

 a member." Membership organizations by nature are designed to let some people in and keep some people out. Zombies, on the other hand, are the ultimate egalitarians. So when I saw an undead Groucho Marx shuffle by me at a zombie walk one summer after-

noon, it hit me that the unique appeal of zombies may be that they are the only club that accepts everyone.

Zombies don't care what you look like. They don't care how old you are. They don't care what you ate last night or if you're cheating on your partner. They don't care if you just got fired or just got a promotion. They don't care about the skeletons in your closet, whether you made the cheerleading squad, or what school you attended. Zombies want you just as much as they want the next guy. They couldn't want you any more or less than they already do. As George Romero puts it, they are the working-class monster.

Zombies are your friends in low places. Everybody is welcome to join their club. So if you don't want to become part of the all-too-welcoming undead horde, you might want to get organized before it's too late!

Zombies never worry that they don't "measure up" as a member of the walking dead. They don't doubt themselves. They don't envy other zombies that are taller, stronger, or have more limbs than they do.

—Z.E.O. *(2009)*, Scott Kenemore

Fortunately or unfortunately, creating a zombie organization is as easy as two guys sitting in their basement with a case of beer asking what they should call their new club. A few clicks of the mouse and they've got a Web site, a Facebook page, and a Twitter account, and are recruiting new members. It happens all the time.

In the past few years, I've watched literally hundreds of zombie organizations come and go. Some look misguided and silly, others seem genuine and worthwhile. Either way, they soon rot back into the earth like the zombies they purport to hunt or protect, research or emulate. If I were to include a complete list of groups in existence as I write this, it would be out of date by the time you read it. Zombie organizations are notorious for launching and dying at lightning pace. But unlike zombies, dead zombie organizations don't rise again.

Here are three major organizations that have stood the test of time. They've proven their worth by developing a dedicated membership and engaging in valuable work.

ZOMBIE RESEARCH SOCIETY (ZRS)

Zombie Research Society (ZRS) was founded in 2007 by a group of academics, artists, and enthusiasts, including me, dedicated to raising the level of zombie scholarship in the arts and sciences. From the beginning, an essential characteristic of ZRS is that we don't make anything up. We don't claim that there was a zombie outbreak last week at a Walmart in Iowa,

 because everyone knows that didn't happen. We don't treat the coming zombie plague as a fictionalized or implausible threat. We ask the simple, scientific questions: If a zombie were to show up at your front door, what would it look like? What would it smell like? How would it hunt you? How would its brain work? From there we extrapolate concrete survival strategies to help overcome the undead plague we may all someday face.

As the Zombie Research Society motto reminds us: what you don't know can eat you.

ZRS members are known as One Percenters because they are committed to being among the 1 percent of people likely to survive a global zombie outbreak. Members come from diverse backgrounds, have different interests, and hold varying theories, but they are unified in their support of the Society's three foundational principles:

1. A zombie is a relentlessly aggressive reanimated human corpse driven by a biological infection.
2. The zombie pandemic is coming. It's not a matter of if, but when.
3. Enthusiastic debate about zombies is essential to the survival of the human race.

Though ZRS was originally conceived as an electronically connected collection of researchers spread across the globe, in 2010, we launched a network of chapters to enable members in local communities to meet each other, host zombie-consciousness-raising activities, and enhance their ability to contend with the undead in their own neighborhoods. Ultimately all zombie catastrophe survival is local, so the ZRS chapter system was a logical next step.

Local chapters host official meetings throughout the year and complete chapter-approved research projects in any of the core ZRS focus areas. Past and ongoing projects include organizing zombie walks and other events, producing zombie-themed work in the arts or media, conducting research on the abilities and dangers of a zombie outbreak, and developing alternate evacuation strategies to be used in a zombie outbreak. Membership in ZRS is available to all, local chapter participation is entirely voluntary, and new chapters are welcome to organize.

ZRS has an advisory board that includes a number of leaders in zombie arts and scholarship, posts regular research updates online, and hosts the Zombie Safehouse, a members-only social network that includes member profile pages, discussion forums, and local chapter pages.

ZOMBIE RESEARCH SOCIETY AWARDS

Launched in 2008 to celebrate the forty-year anniversary of the first lurch of the modern zombie into public consciousness, the ZRS Awards consist of three annual prizes given to individuals, groups, or institutions that have done the most to raise the level of zombie scholarship in the popular culture, sciences, and preparedness, respectively.

In addition, ZRS established the Romero Prize in 2009 to acknowledge one group or individual who has shown great originality, vision, and innovation in their work on zombies in any field. Named in honor of the godfather of the modern zombie and Zombie Research Society board member, George A. Romero, this prize represents the highest honor that ZRS can bestow.

Some past prize winners include the following:

The Walking Dead

The Walking Dead is a dramatic TV series based on Robert Kirkman's graphic novel of the same name. The show takes a serious look at the real-world problems of living through a catastrophic zombie pandemic and has been widely praised by critics and audiences alike. Winner of the 2010 Romero Prize.

"The Living Dead Brain"

The work of neuroscience team Bradley Voytek and Timothy Verstynen represents a major advance in zombie research, resulting in their paper on zombie brain function, "The Living Dead Brain." The pair also developed a three-dimensional theoretical model of a zombie brain. Winner of the 2010 ZRS Award in Science.

Mathematical Zombie Outbreak Modeling

In 2009, a team of researchers from the University of Ottawa published "Mathematical Modeling of an Outbreak of Zombie Infection." It found that a large-scale zombie outbreak would lead to certain doom unless attacked quickly and aggressively. The paper received widespread attention and was named a top idea of the year by the *New York Times.* Winner of the 2009 ZRS Award in Science.

Zombie Haiku

Ryan Mekum's *Zombie Haiku* is the story of one zombie's gradual decay told through poetry. Upon the release of the book, Robert Kirkman said that Mecum had "quite possibly found the only corner of entertainment not yet infected by the zombie plague." Though zombies continue to penetrate further into the pop culture landscape, *Zombie Haiku* stands out for its original take on the classic zombie outbreak scenario. Winner of the 2008 ZRS Award in the Arts.

LOST ZOMBIES

Lost Zombies (LZ) is a zombie-themed social network whose goal is to create the world's first community-generated zombie movie. Intended to be a documentary-style film that chronicles a catastrophic zombie outbreak in the days following complete societal collapse, LZ members create their own online profile pages and are encouraged to submit photos, videos, and audio recordings as well as take part in chat discussions to be used in the eventual feature film.

In 2009, Lost Zombies won the Zombie Research Society Romero Prize for achievement in zombie popular culture. That same year the site earned top honors in both the Social Network and People's Choice categories at the South by SouthWest Web Awards presented as part of the celebrated South by Southwest Interactive festival in Austin, Texas. LZ cofounder Skot Leach says that zombies are the perfect platform to allow an audience to make its own film:

> Zombie outbreaks in movies always start local but inevitably they turn global, so in the long run they impact everyone. We all become part of the same human community fighting to stay alive, and that shared experience gives us a common creative language to make a movie.

Lost Zombies is in good company. Two years before it launched, Twitter was a little-known online application that won its own South by Southwest Web Award in 2007. The resulting attention it received sparked its meteoric transformation into the microblogging behemoth it is today.

Driven by user submissions, Lost Zombies has produced several mobile applications and books, a short film, and other

Web and print products. They are committed to completing their feature film, and I for one can't wait to see it!

ZOMBIE SQUAD (ZS)

Created in 2003 in St. Louis, Missouri, Zombie Squad (ZS) is a nonprofit organization that uses the model of a zombie pandemic to encourage the public to seek education and training necessary to survive a wide range of natural and man-made disasters. ZS works with a number of charities on fund-raisers, food drives, blood drives, and other activities, and was the winner of the 2008 ZRS Award in Preparedness.

Their stated goal is to instruct the public in disaster preparedness in an entertaining way that accounts for multiple worst-case scenarios. Zombie Squad has a strong membership base primarily in North America, as well as an online forum that houses the bulk of their disaster preparedness and survival information.

Zombie Squad is best known for their annual camping weekend called Zombie Con, which kicked off in 2005. Set in rural Irondale, Missouri, Zombie Con is a members-only event that consists of educational survival seminars, trips to a local shooting range, zombie movie screenings, and general outdoor activities such as hiking and canoeing.

37: THE WRONG AND RIDICULOUS

The Aghori is a cannibalistic Hindu sect believed by some to derive mystical powers from their strange and macabre rituals. They live in cemeteries across India, robbing the graves of the newly deceased and then eating the stolen corpses, both raw and cooked on open flames. Their activities are highly illegal, but police are often afraid to intervene.

One Aghori practitioner described eating the dead and bloated body of a pregnant woman, saying that it tasted like mango as chunks of flesh pulled away from her bones. Another recounted eating the brains of the recently dead with his young son:

> I used to wait at the funeral pyre until the skull would burst—
> it bursts with a fine pop—and then I would rapidly, to avoid
> burning my fingers, pull out parts of the brain, which would be
> a gooey mess, partially roasted by then, and would eat it.[74]

By their own account, the Aghori can make skeletons rise and fight each other, and it is said that they use ghosts and demons to take control of the minds of innocent victims.

Their behavior is disturbing and creepy, to be sure, but the Aghori have no connection to the living zombie of contemporary popular culture, much less the undead modern zombie. And they're not even remotely connected to the Haitian voodoo zombie. However, some scholars incorrectly assign the term *zombie* to this sect and its followers.

Varying interpretations and beliefs about the modern zombie are to be expected and can often advance the level of respect and understanding that zombies receive. But there is another category of zombie scholarship that is not driven by honest and intelligent differences of opinion but rather by pure laziness. The authors of such works don't bother to learn much about zombies, familiar-ize themselves with existing zombie research, or even confirm their facts. Indeed, some don't even bother to watch the films or read the books they discuss and reference. Misinformation of this kind only increases widespread confusion about the origins and defin-ing characteristics of the modern zombie and shows a com-plete lack of respect for the subgenre as a whole and for its creator, George A. Romero.

I feel compelled to include some of the most egregious factual errors I've spotted in the published works of zombie critics and scholars. Ultimately, it was the sloppy scholarship seen in the examples below that drove me to write this book and still make me want to stick a fork in my eye every time I come across them. This chapter isn't an extensive catalog of errors, as there are dozens more that I chose not to include because they might be explained away as oversights, typos, or simply honest mistakes.

To be clear, my intention isn't to make anyone look like an idiot, even if they're making grossly idiotic claims. So I've removed the authors' names and publication titles to protect the guilty.

Here is a selected tour of the wrong and ridiculous in recent zombie works of nonfiction:

Quote #1: *The Romero zombie has a fiendish desire for fresh human flesh, in particular warm blood and brains, and will stop at nothing in pursuit of them.*

Correction: Zombies have never eaten brains, said "brains," or shown any interest in brains in any of George Romero's movies. The only zombies in film that eat brains appear in the *Return of the Living Dead* series, which is not part of the Romero franchise. And warm blood? Where did that come from? There are no zombies in any of Romero's films that demonstrate a particular interest in blood, warm or cold. Sadly, this statement was written by a widely published zombie expert who is apparently unfamiliar with Romero's work.

Quote #2: *One of the most entertaining ways of doing this [depicting zombies eating brains] is to show the zombie slicing the top off the victim's head, putting its hands inside it, and eating the still-warm brains.*

Correction: I've never seen, read, or heard of this scenario in any zombie movie, book, or game ever produced. When has a zombie sliced off the top of a person's head and reached in with its hands? What would the zombie use to slice a human skull? And this quote is from a zombie book that bills itself as a "complete guide."

Quote #3: *Moreover, the Romero zombie feels no pain, and therefore will not suffer in the least when set alight. Thus it is unclear how to kill the Romero zombie.*

Correction: Romero made it very clear in his first film, 1968's *Night of the Living Dead*, and in every movie he has made since, that zombies are killed by destroying the brain. Furthermore, the zombies in *Night* are clearly afraid of being set on fire. They back away from flames as survivors set furniture alight to keep them at bay. It makes me wonder if the "zombie expert" who authored these lines has ever seen a zombie movie.

Quote #4: *Mary Shelley's novel,* Frankenstein, *published in 1818, told the tale of a monster who was created from a reanimated corpse, much like a zombie.*

Correction: The monster in Mary Shelley's novel is created by a misguided scientist, Dr. Victor Frankenstein, who gets the bright idea to sew together body parts taken from many different dead people, not a single corpse. Ever wonder why the monster has stitches all over its body? By contrast, zombies are the remains of a single person reanimated by a biological infection. There's a fundamental difference. You'd think this wouldn't have escaped the notice of a published university scholar with several advanced degrees.

Quote #5: *When Johnny senses Barbara's growing anxiety, he reverts to the same puerile behavior, mischievously invoking Boris Karloff, lisp intact, and uttering* Night's *signature line, "They're coming to get you, Barbara."*

Correction: It's Barbra, not Barbara. You might chalk this up to a simple typo, but in a book entirely focused on one movie, *Night of the Living Dead,* is it asking too much that they spell the female lead's name correctly? It is misspelled not once or twice but throughout the entire text. The author also credits John Russo as the sole screenwriter of *Night*, when the film was actually cowritten by Russo and George Romero, based on a Romero short story.

Quote #6: *In 2007, Damon Lemay's* Zombie Town *achieved some acclaim when he portrayed a town of dead people, resurrected and motivated by a mysterious parasite.*

Correction: Some acclaim? Really? I can't find a single film critic who has ever mentioned this movie, let alone given it acclaim. The one review I did hunt down is from an obscure Australian blog stating that *Zombie Town* doesn't have a single shred of originality in it. What's worse, given the dozens of popular, influential, or acclaimed zombie movies in existence, *Zombie Town* is one of only three movies not made by George Romero listed in this book entirely about zombies!

Quote #7: *This [a virus] has killed almost 90 percent of the world's population, only to resurrect them as flesh-eating zombies who can only travel at night or in the shadows.*

Correction: Where do I start with this one? A professional film critic is talking about the Will Smith blockbuster *I Am Legend*, correctly noting that the creatures can't stand sunlight. But she doesn't connect the painfully obvious dots that this is a defining characteristic of vampires, not zombies. I can only assume she hasn't read Richard Matheson's original vampire novel, also titled *I Am Legend*, on which the film is based.

Quote #8: *Although the remake [of* Dawn of the Dead*] had mixed critical reviews, it was a commercial success and remains one of the top-grossing American horror films.*

Correction: Zack Snyder's remake of *Dawn of the Dead* is not one of the top-grossing American horror films. It wasn't even one of the top-three-grossing horror movies the year it was released (2004). It claimed fourth place at best, behind *The Grudge, Saw,* and another zombie movie, *Resident Evil: Apocalypse.* What's more, it wasn't even the top-grossing horror remake to hit theaters within six months of its release. That honor went to *The Texas Chainsaw Massacre.*

Quote #9: *[In* Night of the Living Dead*] a number of teenagers are trapped in a remote and abandoned farmhouse by a group of these mobile corpses who are hungry for their flesh.*

Correction: There are no teenagers in *Night of the Living Dead.* The two leads, Ben and Barbra, are thirty-two and twenty-three, respectively. The next two most prominent characters trapped in the farmhouse are a married couple in their forties. Even their daughter, the young girl who famously turns into a zombie in the film, is just eleven. This hogwash comes from a two-hundred-plus-page book with *Zombies* in the title that has just three pages devoted to anything related to the modern zombie. And still its facts are all wrong.

Now that I've had my say on the wrong and ridiculous, I ask that you keep a skeptical eye open and check out the validity of what you read on zombies. Junk gets published every day. Just because something is in print doesn't mean it's accurate, remotely factual, or even worth the paper it's printed on.

And if you're going to write about zombies, please take the time to confirm your claims. Resist the urge to make sloppy comparisons or sweeping generalizations. And at the very least, watch the films and read the books you're writing about. Seriously, people.

38: FINAL THOUGHTS

If you take just one thing from this book, I hope it's a belief that the modern zombie has earned the right to be recognized and clearly defined.

Filled with pure aggression, limited in its biological makeup, and driven by an infection that threatens to swallow the whole of the human race, Romero's flesh eater is fundamentally the same creature today as it was when it first appeared in *Night of the Living Dead* in 1968. It also continues to prove remarkably relevant through the changing decades.

The modern zombie evolved from vampires, not from the soulless voodoo slaves that share their name. But unlike vampires, the walking dead don't carry with them the baggage of Old World superstitions and myths. They aren't supernatural, superhuman, superstrong, or particularly super at anything. Just the opposite. Zombies are grossly natural in their rotting flesh, imperfect brains, and limited physical abilities. They don't pretend to be anything more or less than what they are.

But what they are is the end of the world.

MORE QUESTIONS THAN ANSWERS

All zombie research is theoretical. We can never know exactly what the coming pandemic will look like until the teeming undead horde is finally at our doorsteps.

You may think that day will never come, and you could be right. But as Daniel Drezner, professor of international politics at Tufts University, argues, even if the chance of a zombie pandemic is a fraction of 1 percent, it represents such a profound and devastating threat to modern civilization that the only responsible course of action is intense research and preparation.[75] Because once the dead rise, the days of study and conjecture are over.

Gone will be reasoned debate and hard scientific study. Gone will be global lines of communication and easy access to information. Gone will be the support structures that allow us to engage easily in serious scientific, social, and historic investigation. When the dead rise, it's run-and-scream time.

Therefore, mankind's research goal must be to develop solid working theories that foster as complete an understanding as possible of the dangers we face before it's too late.

ALL SURVIVAL IS LOCAL

The steps it takes to survive the aftermath of a large-scale zombie outbreak are much the same as those needed to survive any prolonged catastrophic natural or man-made disaster.

Our basic human requirements remain constant, and attention to those requirements means the difference between life and death. In survivalist circles, this simple and well-established principle is known as the Rule of Three, which holds that in a worst-case scenario, a person can live only so long without certain essentials.

In three minutes, you're dead without air.
In three hours, you're dead without shelter.
In three days, you're dead without water.
In three weeks, you're dead without food.

If you live in a mild climate, you may think you don't need immediate protection from the elements, but you will always need protection from roaming zombies and the other deadly threats outlined in the previous chapters.

Most importantly, don't get lost in fantasies of video-game action or big-screen gore. No weapons compound is wailing for you to claim its stash. No armored car is gassed up and ready to lead you out of town. There is no pause in a real zombie outbreak. No reset button when the undead overrun your defenses. No extra lives when you reach your destination, only to be shot in the back by a panicked friend or stranger.

When the dead walk, one mistake is one too many.

THE CLOCK IS TICKING

Finally, clinging to rigid preconceived notions about the living dead is a recipe for disaster.

No one can tell you exactly how zombies will behave or exactly what impact the chaos and panic they incite will have on civilization. Following the strict advice of others who claim to have all the answers will likely get you killed and eaten in the first days of the coming zombie pandemic. For me, I'm not interested in being right. I'm interested in staying alive.

So don't trust what I say as fact. Don't blindly trust any published expert. Don't even trust yourself, as ego and bias can be deadly hazards. Do the work. Learn the facts. Develop new theories that might save the planet from the zombie menace. Contribute to the mounting research efforts going on across the globe.

Because what you don't know can eat you.

NOTES

Note: All uncited quotes in this book come from the author's direct communication with the people involved.

1. *Variety*, October 16, 1968.
2. *Reader's Digest*, June 1969.
3. Jonathan Maberry, *Zombie CSU: The Forensics of the Living Dead*.
4. Jamie Russell, *Book of the Dead: The Complete History of Zombie Cinema*.
5. "Getting Beyond Myra and the Valley of the Junk," *New York Times*, July 5, 1970.
6. Spike TV 2009 Scream Awards.
7. Mike Bruno, "John Carpenter: The Sultan of Scare," ew.com, October 23 2007.
8. From the film *Targets*, Saticoy Productions, 1968.
9. Joe Kane, *Night of the Living Dead: Behind the Scenes of the Most Terrifying Zombie Movie Ever*.
10. *Last Man on Earth* (1964), *Omega Man* (1971), and *I Am Legend* (2007).
11. Rock 'N' Tattoo at http://rockntattooandpiercing.com.
12. Jonathan Maberry, *Zombie CSU: The Forensics of the Living Dead*.
13. Moviefone Interview, February 16, 2008.
14. Honda's ASIMO robot stands just four feet, three inches tall and weighs 119 pounds.
15. Bradley Voytek and Timothy Verstynen, "The Living Dead Brain," paper presented at ZomBcon in Seattle, October 30, 2010.
16. *Science Newsline*, March 11, 2010.
17. *Science Daily*, March 3, 2008.
18. "On the Levy-Walk Nature of Human Mobility," North Carolina State University study.
19. Kathryn Lord, "Not Only Dogs, but Deer, Monkeys and Birds Bark to Deal with Conflict," *Science Daily*, July 15, 2009.
20. Rita Carter, *The Human Brain Book*.
21. Jonathan Maberry, *Zombie CSU: The Forensics of the Living Dead*.
22. "The Truth Behind Zombies," National Geographic Channel, October 30, 2010.

23. Patricia Gadsby, "Why Mosquitoes Suck," *Discover*, August 1, 1997.
24. John Tayman, *The Colony: The Harrowing True Story of the Exiles of Molokai.*
25. Lisa Grossman, "All Life on Earth Could Have Come from Alien Zombies," *Wired Science*, November 10, 2010.
26. "Infectious Prions Capable of Darwinian Evolution," *Drug Discovery and Development*, January 4, 2010.
27. "Swine Flu Pandemic Strain Still Mutating," *H1N1 News*, July 18, 2010.
28. "The Truth Behind Zombies," National Geographic Channel, October 30, 2010.
29. "Rutgers Cell Biologist Pinpoints How RNA Viruses Copy Themselves," National Science Foundation news, www.nsf.gov, May 28, 2010.
30. Daniel Robert Epstein, "Zack Snyder Talks *Dawn of the Dead*," Ugo.com, undated 2004 interview. Accessed January 10, 2011.
31. Daniel Wójcik, *The End of the World as We Know It: Faith, Fatalism, and Apocalypse in America.*
32. Andy Coghlan, "Planned U.S. Bio-Lab Is Riskier Than Officials Say," *New Scientist*, November 18, 2010.
33. "Tamiflu Ban for Teens to Continue," Kyoto News section, *Japan Times*, June 5, 2009.
34. Centers for Disease Control and Prevention, December 21, 2009.
35. Donald G. McNeil, Jr., "Desperate Addicts Inject Others' Blood," *New York Times*, July 12, 2010.
36. Wynne Parry, "New Zombie-Ant Fungi Found," *Live Science*, March 2, 2011.
37. "The Science of Mind Control," www.tonsandtons.wordpress.com, July 20, 2010.
38. Pete Nelson, *Left for Dead: A Young Man's Search for Justice for the USS Indianapolis.*
39. National Public Radio, January 12, 2011.
40. Shane Painter, *The Urban Survivalist Handbook.*
41. Richard W. Wrangham, *Catching Fire: How Cooking Made Us Human.*
42. *NBC Nightly News*, February 28, 2010.
43. *The 700 Club* with Pat Robertson, Christian Broadcasting Network, January 13, 2010.
44. Ian McGregor, "Reactive Approach Motivation for Religion," *Journal of Personality and Social Psychology*, July 2010.
45. James F. Miskel, *Disaster Response and Homeland Security: What Works, What Doesn't.*

46. *Shreveport Times*, March 7, 2010.
47. Jonah Lehrer, "Stress," www.scienceblogs.com, July 19, 2010.
48. Vaughan Bell, "Frequency and Predictors of Mass Psychogenic Illness," *Epidemiology*, September 21, 2010.
49. Michele Rosenthal, http://healmyptsd.com, June 8, 2010.
50. Albert D. Biderman, "The Manipulation of Human Behavior."
51. Peter Landers, "Japanese Plant Had Barebones Risk Plan," *The Wall Street Journal*, March 31, 2011.
52. Simon Pegg on *Shaun of the Dead*, www.cinecon.com.
53. Ali Khan, "Preparedness 101: Zombie Apocalypse," Centers for Disease Control and Prevention, www.emergency.cdc.gov, May 16, 2011.
54. "Are You Ready?" www.fema.gov, November 3, 2010.
55. Nicholas DiFonzo, *The Watercooler Effect: A Psychologist Explores the Extraordinary Power of Rumors*.
56. Dave Grossman, *On Killing: The Psychological Cost of Learning to Kill in War and Society*.
57. Amy Gahran, "Why You Need a Zombie Apocalypse Phone," CNN.com, August 27, 2010.
58. John M. Barry, *The Great Influenza: The Story of the Deadliest Pandemic in History*.
59. Hadley Leggett, "Universal Death Stench Repels Bugs of All Types," *Wired*, www.wired.com, September 11, 2009.
60. Lawrence Stager, "An Investigation into the Roanoke Colony," *Harvard Alumni Magazine*, August 17, 2009.
61. Christine Dell-Amore, History, Mystery in Ancient Lead Sarcophagus," www.foxnews.com, March 31, 2010.
62. "Headless Gladiator Graveyard Unearthed," www.news.discovery.com, July 7, 2010.
63. "Americans' Job Satisfaction Falls to Record Low," Associated Press, January 5, 2010.
64. Gustav Janouch, *Conversations with Kafka*.
65. "Sam Raimi Says George Romero Inspired Him," www.horror-movies.ca, May 13, 2009.
66. Joe Kane, *Night of the Living Dead: Behind the Scenes of the Most Terrifying Zombie Move Ever*.
67. *Washington Times*, August 26, 2010.
68. Tim Molloy, "*Walking Dead* Finale Scores Record Ratings for AMC," www.thewrap.com, December 6, 2010.
69. Ain't It Cool News, www.aintitcool.com, May 26, 2010.
70. Planet of Terror, www.planetofterror.com, July 13, 2010.
71. Empire Online, www.empireonline.com, April 27, 2011.

72. Alex Navarro, "*Land of the Dead* Review," www.gamespot.com, February 10, 2006.

73. Dean Robbins, "Out for Blood, Zombies Protest Gov. Scott Walker at Wisconsin Capitol," www.thedailypage.com, April 2, 2011.

74. Paul Raffaele, *Among the Cannibals*.

75. Daniel W. Drezner, *Theories of International Politics and Zombies*.